Johanna Thiel

P9-BBQ-305

Boxers

Everything about Purchase, Care, Nutrition, Breeding, Behavior, and Training

Translated by Kathleen Luft

With 27 color photos
by Christine Steimer

Drawings by Renate Holzner

Consulting Editor:
Matthew M. Vriends, Ph.D.

BARRON'S

Contents

This boxer waits tensely to see what is about to happen; in any event, it is prepared to jump.

In the role of guard, the boxer is completely in its element.

Preface

Scarcely any other dog can produce such inimitable wrinkles upon its forehead as the boxer, and scarcely any other dog gazes at you so good-naturedly while furrowing its brow. In fact, the boxer is an affectionate dog with a deep attachment to its human family and a fundamentally playful temperament.

In this Barron's Complete Pet Owner's Manual, Johanna Thiel, who has raised and lived with boxers for many years, introduces this energy-filled family pet and gives guidelines—based on her long experience—to its proper care. She describes the origin of the breed, gives a detailed explanation of the breed standard and provides easy-to-understand tips on acquiring a boxer and getting it settled into your home. Before discussing the fundamentals of both basic and more specialized dog training, she describes, with great sensitivity, the typical behavior patterns of the breed. There are practical suggestions on proper grooming, a healthy diet, and preventive health care for boxers. Also included is a brief introduction to breeding and to showing your pet.

The graphic drawings of Renate Holzner on the informative how-to pages, and Christine Steimer's photos, taken exclusively for this pet manual, give an impressive picture of the boxer.

The author and the editors wish you a great deal of pleasure with your boxer.

The Typical Boxer

Breed Characteristics

"If the boxer didn't exist, we would have to invent one!" What other dog can make such wrinkles appear upon its forehead? What other dog can look at you so faithfully that you simply can't be angry at it? Often boxers are called the philosophers of the dog world. That may be attributable to the fact that they frequently seem somewhat dreamy and absentminded, yet the next instant they can be fully alert and ready to protect their family from anything.

The character of a dog is made up of instincts and hereditary factors, with all the modifications brought about by environmental influences. Typical of the boxer's nature, and definitely its most prominent feature, is the juxtaposition of very different sets of traits. These traits, however, coexist in complete harmony: On the one hand, the boxer exhibits fearlessness and unflinching courage. It is self-assured and possesses high spirits and energy in equal measure. Its alertness is legendary. On the other hand, it also is characterized by pronounced affection and loyalty where its significant human and all other family members are concerned. Its special characteristics also include its playfulness, which persists well into old age. Moreover, it loves children and cannot be bribed by strangers. All these qualities make the boxer easy to keep as a pet, despite its size, and an ideal dog for a family. If opposite characteristics are displayed, they are faults of that particular boxer, and they must be interpreted as defects in that dog's character.

Because of its pronounced liveliness and desire for activity, the boxer needs a great deal of attention and involvement on the part of its owner.

Origin of the Breed

Boxers have a long history that goes back to ancient times. From his Indian campaign, Alexander the Great brought home huge dogs of the old mastiff type whose distinguishing feature was their wide mouth. By contrast, the other dogs of antiquity had pointed mouths. The dogs brought back by Alexander probably formed the initial basis for the breeding of Molossian hounds. This breed's name came from its origin in the Greek province in which the Molossian royal family ruled. Later, dogs of such origin also came into use by the Romans. They were considered invincible until the "Britannic mastiffs," huge British fighting dogs, appeared on the scene. They had an even broader mouth and even greater strength than the Molossian dogs, and for that reason they gradually replaced the Molossians. From then on the two breeds were crossed with each other, though their offspring continued to bear the name of Molossian hounds. These dogs are one ancestral line of our present-day boxer.

The second line is represented by the mastiffs, which were bred from the British fighting dogs. Their appearance, size, and body weight varied, depending on the purpose for which they were used.

The third line developed among the Celts and Germanic tribes. They too bred large dogs that were unusually rugged and powerful. Central Europe produced the large, or Danzig, "bullenbeisser" (bull biter) and the small, or

Boxers can furrow their brow in inimitable fashion.

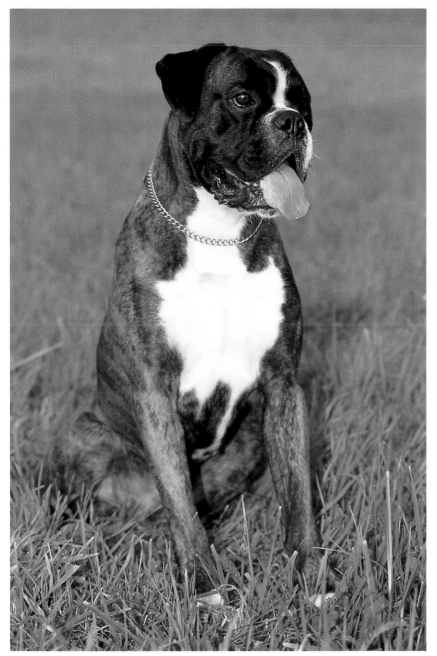

In a boxer, very dissimilar character traits coexist in harmony: affectionate, but fearlessly courageous at the same time, the boxer is a good-natured playmate, but a stern guard and protector.

A boxer with a brindle coat and white markings on its chest and mask.

Brabant, bullenbeisser. This lighter bullenbeisser is considered the immediate ancestor of today's boxers.

The Direct Ancestors

In those days the breeding of the bullenbeisser was mostly under the control of hunters who performed their services exclusively for ruling houses. It was the bullenbeisser's job to seize the game driven by the tracking hounds and hang onto the animal until the hunter came and killed his quarry. For this task, the dog needed as wide a mouth as possible, with a broad bite. Only thus equipped could it get a firm grip with its teeth and then hold tightly to its quarry. Through breeding, the upper jaw became progressively shortened. The result was the protrusive occlusion that allowed the dog enough room to breathe while holding on to the quarry. This overbite is typical of the boxer.

Efforts to Improve the Breed

Breeding of pedigreed boxers did not begin in Germany until the second half of the eighteenth century. The bullenbeisser of the eighteenth century did not yet represent a uniform type. Many of them were mongrels or were crossed with bulldogs. Nonetheless, there was a centuries-long tradition of linebreeding with the bullenbeisser. That made it possible to work on developing a uniform type. The name "boxer" for this uniform type first made its appearance between 1860 and 1870. A little later, in 1895, some proponents of linebreeding of boxers joined together to found a boxer club in Munich. It was they who also made the Munich "beer boxer" of their day into the popular family pet and utility dog known today. Today it is very hard to imagine how difficult that was to accomplish, in the absence of any knowledge of genetics and of bloodlines.

Another of the achievements of the newly founded boxer club was the authoritative establishment of the breed standard. Previously breeding had been based solely on a practical point of view: Matings took place in accordance with the intended use. Now there existed a guideline independent of that practice, a guideline to which breeders as well as judges could adhere.

One of the first boxer kennels to make a name for itself with its breeding program was vom Dom. The owner, Friderun Stockmann, thus laid the basis for a boxer strain that was highly respected in Germany and elsewhere. From it came the legendary Lustig vom Dom. Many of today's boxers are descended from that stud.

The first United States boxer was registered in 1904. An import, the famous Sieger Dampf von Dom became the first United States champion in 1915. This dog was owned by Herbert H. Lehman, who later became the governor of New York State. Popularity of the breed skyrocketed when Ch. Warlord of Mazelaine went best in show at the 1947 Westminster Kennel Club competition.

The AKC Breed Standard

The standard for a dog breed describes in ideal terms all the features a representative of that breed should possess. The specifications of the breed standard, which are obligatory, are always laid down in a studbook. They must be adhered to in breeding. At the same time, these guidelines serve the judges at dog shows as a basis for their scoring.

The studbook also contains a record of all the breeding particulars. Thus it supplies the family tree for the entire breed, and for each puppy from a breeding program it is possible to call up the entire gallery of its forebears.

The studbook is, so to speak, a marriage license register for dogs.

General Appearance

The boxer is a medium-sized, square-built dog of good substance with a short back, strong limbs, and a short, tight-fitting coat. Its well-developed muscles are clean and hard and appear smooth under taut skin. Its movements should denote energy. The gait is firm, yet elastic, the stride free and ground covering, the carriage proud. Developed to serve as a guard, working, and companion dog, the boxer combines strength and agility with elegance and style. Its expression is alert and its temperament is steadfast and tractable.

The boxer's chiseled head is a unique individual stamp. It must be in correct proportion to the body. The broad, blunt muzzle is its most distinctive feature, with great value placed upon proper form and balance with the skull.

In judging the boxer, first consideration should be given to general appearance to which attractive color and arresting style contribute; next, overall balance with special attention to the head, after which the individual body components are examined for their correct construction, and efficiency of gait is evaluated.

Height, Proportion, Substance

Height: Adult males 22.5 to 25 inches (57–63.5 cm); females 21 to 23.5 inches (53–59.7 cm) at the withers. Preferably, males should not be under the minimum nor females over the maximum; however, proper balance and quality in the individual should be of primary importance because there is no size disqualification.

Proportion: The body in profile is of square proportion in that a horizontal line from the front of the forechest to the rear projection of the upper thigh should equal the length of a vertical line dropped from the top of the withers to the ground.

Substance: Sturdy with balanced musculature. Males are larger boned than their female counterparts.

Boxers practice typical behavioral patterns as they play together. Here the boxer on the left is challenging the one on the right to a make-believe fight.

The mother dog patiently puts up with the rowdy behavior of her puppies. While tussling with their litter-mates, the puppies learn movements and patterns of behavior.

Head

The beauty of the head depends upon the harmonious proportion of the muzzle to the skull. The blunt muzzle is one third the length of the head from the occiput to the tip of the nose, and two thirds the width of the skull. The head should be clean, not showing deep wrinkles (wet). Wrinkles typically appear upon the forehead when ears are erect, and folds are always present from the lower edge of the stop running downward on both sides of the muzzle.

Expression: Intelligent and alert.

Eyes: Dark brown in color, not too small, too protruding, or too deep set. Their mood-mirroring character combined with the wrinkling of the forehead, gives the boxer head its unique quality of expressiveness.

Ears: Set at the highest points of the sides of the skull are cropped, cut rather long and tapering, raised when alert.

Skull: The top of the skull is slightly arched, not rounded, flat, nor noticeable broad, with the occiput not overly

pronounced. The forehead shows a slight indentation between the eyes and forms a distinct stop with the topline of the muzzle.

Muzzle: The muzzle, proportionately developed in length, width, and depth, has a shape influenced through the formation of both jawbones, the placement of the teeth, and the texture of the lips. The nose should be broad and black.

The upper jaw is broad where attached to the skull and maintains this breadth except for a very slight tapering to the front. The lips should meet evenly in front. The upper lip is thick and padded, filling out the frontal space created by the projection of the lower jaw, and laterally is supported by the canines of the lower jaw. Therefore, these canines must stand far apart and are of good length so that the front surface of the muzzle is broad and squarish.

Bite: The boxer bite is undershot; the lower jaw protrudes beyond the upper and curves slightly upward. The incisor teeth of the lower jaw are in a straight line, with the canines preferably up front in the same line to give the jaw the greatest possible width.

Faults: Skull too broad. Cheekiness. Wrinkling too deep (wet) or lacking (dry). Excessive flews. Muzzle too light for skull. Too pointed a bite (snippy), too undershot, teeth or tongue showing when mouth closed. Eyes noticeably lighter than ground color of coat.

Neck, Topline, Body

Neck: Round, of ample length, muscular, and clean without excessive hanging skin (dewlap). The neck has a distinctly marked nape with an elegant arch blending smoothly into the withers.

Topline: Smooth, firm, and slightly sloping.

A brindle male boxer, as specified in the breed standard.

Body: The chest is of fair width, and the forechest is well defined and visible from the side. The back is short, straight, and muscular and firmly connects the withers to the hindquarters. The loins are short and muscular. The lower stomach line is slightly tucked up, blending into a graceful curve to the rear. The croup is slightly sloped, flat, and broad. The tail is set high, docked, and carried upward. The pelvis is long and in females especially broad.

Faults: Short heavy neck. Chest too broad, too narrow, or hanging between the shoulders. Lack of forechest. Hanging stomach. Slab-sided rib cage. Long or narrow loin, weak union with croup. Falling off of croup. Higher in rear than in front.

Coat

Short, shiny, lying smooth and tight to the body.

Color

The colors are fawn and brindle. Fawn shades vary from light tan to mahogany. The brindle ranges from sparse, but clearly defined black stripes on a fawn background, to such a heavy concentration of black striping that the essential fawn background color barely, although clearly, shows through (which may create the appearance of reverse brindling). White markings should be of such distribution as to enhance the dog's appearance, but may not exceed one third of the entire coat. They are not desirable on the flanks or on the back of the torso proper. On the face, white may replace part of the otherwise essential black mask and may extend in an upward path between the eyes, but it must not be excessive, so as to detract from a true boxer expression.

Faults: Unattractive or misplaced white markings.

Gait

Proper front and rear angulation is manifested in a smoothly efficient, level-backed, ground-covering stride with powerful drive emanating from a freely operating rear. Although the front legs do not contribute impelling power, adequate reach should be evident to prevent interference, overlap, or sidewinding (crabbing).

Faults: Stilted or inefficient gait. Lack of smoothness.

Character and Temperament

The breed standard also specifies the boxer's character and temperament. Accordingly, the boxer should be courageous, self-confident, calm, and even tempered. The typical boxer is affectionate and loyal in dealing with family members, but mistrustful of strangers; cheerful and friendly at play, but fearless when things get serious.

Left, a boxer with a normal stance, viewed from the rear. The dog in the center has bandy legs; the boxer on the right is cow-hocked.

Tips on Buying a Boxer

When you buy a boxer you are assuming a great responsibility, because the dog is totally at the mercy of its owner. Before you decide to purchase a boxer, therefore, you need to think about a few things:

• A boxer's life expectancy is about 10 to 12 years. Can you guarantee that your pet will be well cared for in your household for that length of time?

• Do your living conditions meet the requirements of such an animal? Not everyone who decides to buy a boxer has to have a house with a yard—although that would be ideal. Boxers also can be kept very easily in an apartment or condo (if exercised daily), because they are quiet dogs. However, the apartment should not be small, because boxers have a great need for activity and require a corresponding degree of freedom of movement.

• To keep a dog in a rented apartment, you need the written agreement of the landlord, in advance.

• The issue of "going outdoors" is particularly important where a rented apartment is concerned. Is there a vacant area in the immediate vicinity where the boxer can relieve itself? If there is not, you may possibly have to drive several miles to find a suitable spot.

• Who will look after your boxer when you go on vacation? Do you have in mind destinations to which your dog could easily accompany you?

Before buying a boxer, ask yourself: Will a boxer fit into my life—and into my home?

Licenses and Insurance

If you have made the decision to buy a boxer, you have to keep the following in mind as well:

• In most areas, buying a dog license is one of the duties of the dog owner. You must report your dog—puppies, too—to the local authorities within ten days after you get it.

• In addition, it is advisable to take out liability insurance for your dog. It will cover any damage your pet might cause. However, it does not release you from your own duty to be diligent in supervising the dog.

• Health insurance for dogs is also available now (see Useful Addresses and Literature, page 60). Each dog owner must decide individually whether taking out such a policy is advisable.

A Male or a Female?

The question of whether it is more convenient to get a male or a female cannot be answered in a clear-cut way. The gender of your pet—just like its color—is primarily a matter of personal preference. Nonetheless, there are some objective reasons as well that may decide the issue in favor of a certain gender:

A male will be larger, heavier, and stronger than a female. A boxer 25 inches (63.5 cm) high at the withers can reach the considerable weight of about 71 pounds (32 kg). Its size and strength are factors to consider. A fully grown male boxer, because of its boisterous response to other males, can be physically very exhausting for its owner. Here, so-called dominance behavior plays a major role. On the other hand, a male naturally will not bring any unplanned offspring home, even if it

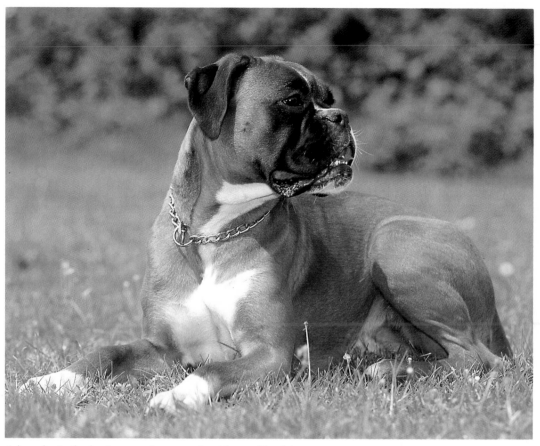

A breeder is the best source for a purebred boxer like this one.

has managed to run off despite careful supervision.

A female, as a rule, is smaller and lighter than a male. She also is usually somewhat more alert; after all, as a mother she has to rear her puppies. However, a female normally is in season twice a year. Many people wish to avoid the minor inconveniences associated with this so-called heat (see The Mating Act, page 56). Suppressing estrus with medications, however, is not advisable. Such treatments often result in subsequent impairment of the dog's health, such as inflammation of the uterus.

A Puppy or an Adult Dog?

Personally, I prefer buying a puppy. That allows me to have some control over its training. If the dog later develops peculiarities nonetheless, then at least they are my own responsibility. When buying an adult dog, you need to find out the precise reasons that led the previous owners to sell their pet. In this way you are better prepared for

The puppy licks the mother dog's chops to show that it wants to be fed.

potential surprises such as inability to get along with other dogs or other peculiarities.

Living with other animals: How well the newly acquired boxer is able to share a household with other pets depends on its age. Certainly a puppy will come to terms with other animals more easily than an adult dog, which may already have had negative experiences. In such cases you need to make sure that each animal acknowledges the other's living space.

One Dog or Two?

A single boxer feels very comfortable as the "supreme ruler" in the family. Its playmates are, by and large, the members of the family. It even prefers them to another dog that is not part of the family. If you want to add a second boxer to your household, keep the following in mind:

• You will have twice the amount of work when it comes to feeding and grooming the dogs.

• Please remember that every dog, whether a loner or part of a pack, is an individual with particular character traits and its own temperament.

• When choosing a vacation site, you need to know whether you can take along the second dog, too.

A second boxer: If a second boxer joins your household, your first pet needs a few days to get used to the new dog. If your pet is already fairly advanced in years, a surprise is. in store for you: The boxer will be rejuvenated.

The fewest problems in adjustment will arise if the new addition and your present boxer form a male-female pair. In any event, the adjustment process is substantially easier for a puppy if there is already another dog in the family.

In a Household with Children

As a family dog, a boxer poses no difficulty in its dealings with children. It is irrelevant whether you have a male or a female. The children need to learn, however, not to treat their boxer as they would a toy or to hurt it. When dealing with puppies in particular, you need to be careful, because puppies are definitely capable of inflicting painful bites and scratches. Always keep an eye on small children when your boxer is present. Then you can intervene at once if the boxer's liveliness when playing, for example, ever gives rise to a threatening situation.

What the Buyer Needs to Know

Once you have decided that a boxer is right for you, the next question, of course, is this: "Where do I get a boxer?" It is best to buy a puppy from a breeder who belongs to the American

Boxer Club (see Useful Addresses and Literature, page 60).

How to Find a Good Breeder

Addresses of reliable boxer breeders are also obtainable from the American Kennel Club (AKC) (see Useful Addresses and Literature on page 60). The AKC also has an excellent video about boxers. This videotape would probably be a very good investment for any potential boxer owner.

There are specialized magazines and newsletters available that deal with boxers (ask your local dog club about these publications). By learning as much as you can about boxer breeders, you will be in a better position to choose the place to obtain your boxer.

Other places to contact:
• In many areas you may find boxer clubs. Talk with the members and get their recommendations of possible sources. There may be a boxer breeders' organization in your city or state. Boxer breeders/exhibitors generally know who among their peers has a litter of pups, an older pet-quality puppy, or an adult boxer in need of a good home. Because these are the people who show dogs, they probably can help you find a pup with dog show potential. Often these boxer clubs have appropriate training sites.
• When you see a boxer owner on the street, don't hesitate to ask him or her about the dog's origin. As a rule, owners are glad to give you the address of their pet's breeder.

Note: It is not a good idea to get a boxer through a puppy mill or mail-order business. In these transactions, the dog is ordered and delivered as freight. Thus, you have no idea in advance how your dog looks or what its parentage is. Consequently, you also receive no pedigree.

How to Choose a Puppy

In choosing a puppy, let your personal taste guide your decision. You have ample time available to make your selection, because a puppy never goes to a new home before its ninth week of life. Until that time you can keep coming back to look over the litter. Naturally it is best if you pick a likely candidate early on. Then you can keep visiting it to play with it. In this way it will have a chance to grow accustomed to you.

In addition to its state of health (see Signs of a Healthy Puppy, following), the puppy's temperament should be an important criterion in making your choice. After all, you would like a dog that suits you and your style of life. Pay close attention to the individual "personalities" in the litter. If you want a lively housemate, pick a puppy that romps boisterously with its littermates and also comes up to you immediately when you visit. If a calmer type is more

Signs of a Healthy Puppy

• The puppy has a thick coat of hair with a silky gloss. It should not be dull and lusterless.
• Its eyes are clear and bright. They should not be dull or tearing.

In addition, a normally developed, healthy puppy is always:
• curious: It will explore its surroundings thoroughly and approach humans with interest. The puppy should not be fearful.
• lively: The puppy is active, moves nimbly, and reacts to all external stimuli. It should not be apathetic.
• playful: The puppy accepts every invitation to play and makes appropriate use of every object offered for play.

apt to appeal to your temperament, then the right puppy for you is the one that is not involved in every tussle and sometimes watches the goings-on with interest from the sidelines. In any event, however, your ideal puppy should be bright and responsive. Don't let yourself be guided by pity to choose a puppy that is poorly socialized. A proper boxer will always be a bundle of energy. Caution is in order if there is any indication of illness or behavioral disturbance.

Advantages of Buying from a Breeder

A reputable breeder of boxers voluntarily adheres to the American Boxer Club's regulations governing purebred dogs and their health; normally the breeder is an amateur and a hobby breeder. If you buy your boxer from a breeder, you will not only be getting an animal that conforms to the breed standard; you also will have the guarantee that the puppy has had the best possible care:
• At the breeder's, the puppies grow up together as a litter, and the imprint-

If it feels contented, the boxer will roll in the grass.

ing phase, which begins after the third week (see Developmental Phases, page 27), in most cases is characterized by human contact and loving rearing.
• With a dog from a breeder, moreover, you have the assurance that it has been well nourished. Because the breeder takes a systematic approach to nutrition, he or she is also able to document precisely what the puppy has been fed.

My tip: At first, feed your puppy exactly what the breeder gave it. Switching to a different food is very difficult for the puppy. If the switch is made too soon, painful gastrointestinal upsets can result. For this reason, have your breeder give you a feeding plan.

Vaccination Certificate and Worming

You have two additional advantages when you buy your boxer from a breeder:
• The puppy has been vaccinated against hepatitis, leptospirosis, distemper, and parvovirus disease (see Vaccination Schedule, page 51). The breeder has this basic series of immunizations performed within the puppy's first eight weeks of life. When the breeding supervisor evaluates the puppies after the eighth week, the breeder also presents him or her with the appropriate proofs of vaccination.
• A reputable boxer breeder also makes sure that the puppies are adequately wormed (see Worming, page 48) before they are released to the buyers beginning with the ninth week of life.

Note: When buying a boxer, therefore, make absolutely sure that you receive the current health records, showing the dates of all vaccinations, worming, and examinations by a licensed veterinarian, including the results and treatments.

Boxers are bundles of energy with enormous stamina.

Sales Contract

Buying a boxer is a matter of confidence. Nevertheless, it is advisable to conclude a contract of sale. Appropriate blank contracts are available from the American Boxer Club as well as from the AKC and the FCI (Fédération Cynologique Internationale). Such an agreement is not a requirement, but it does offer the buyer and the breeder a certain protection.

Pedigree

If you have bought your boxer from a breeder who belongs to the American Boxer Club, you will also receive a pedigree. It is issued by the AKC or the American Boxer Club, because it is the recognized breeders' organization for the boxer. In the proof of descent issued by the club, the animal's name and origin are recorded. The document also certifies that your dog comes from a supervised breeding program of the American Boxer Club and complies with the breed standard as well as the club's breeding regulations (see The AKC Breed Standard, page 6).

With dogs that have some other proof of descent, it is important that the breeders' association in question also be recognized by the FCI. The FCI is the international umbrella organization responsible for supervised breeding of pedigreed dogs (see Useful Addresses and Literature, page 60).

Sources of Danger in Your Home

Naturally your house or apartment contains a number of potential dangers for your puppy. Eliminate these sources of danger before your new pet joins your household.

Basic Equipment for Your Boxer

Collar with leash: One of the first pieces of equipment your boxer needs is a leather collar, which should not be too tight. You can ask your dog's breeder to measure the circumference of the puppy's neck and tell you what size to buy.

In addition, you need a leather leash, or lead, about 6.5 feet (2 m) long and not overly heavy. If roughly one third of the leash's lower portion consists of metal links, it is unsuitable, because puppies try to free themselves from this as yet unfamiliar device by biting on the leash. The metal links, however, will damage the little milk teeth. Also unsuitable are dog leashes that retract automatically. Even a young puppy needs to learn a bit of leash discipline, and this type of leash is not appropriate for such lessons.

When the dog is older, it will need a heavy-duty leather leash that can stand up to its high spirits, as well as a chain-link collar. The latter, also known as a choke collar, tightens when the boxer jerks at its leash.

Dog bed: Your puppy's bed is very important to its sense of well-being. Place the bed in a quiet, draft-free spot where the dog will be undisturbed but will not lack contact with its family. In addition, the spot you choose should not be overly warm—near the central heating, for example. That can potentially lead to out-of-season shedding and make the dog more susceptible to colds. The dog bed itself should not be overly soft. A basket or a mattress would be the best choice. It is a good idea to get a bed large enough to accommodate your boxer even after it is fully grown.

Food dish: You also need a food bowl and a water bowl. Both should be easy to clean. Pet stores sell models that are difficult to overturn and have adjustable heights. Choose a height setting that suits your dog's size, and move the bowls higher as the boxer grows. The advantage of these adjustable devices is that they keep your boxer's forelegs from turning out and becoming bent.

Toys: The puppy also needs playthings. They not only entertain the boxer and provide playful activity, but also keep it from getting interested in furniture and carpets. Good choices are a hard ball or a solid rubber ring.

The ball has to be big enough not to be swallowed by the boxer. Old cotton socks tied in a knot also make an excellent toy. Rubber toys are not appropriate, because the young dog will gnaw on them and might swallow pieces of them. Also unsuitable are all materials that could splinter, including hard plastic, wood, and celluloid.

If you have a puppy, remember it will need to satisfy its chewing urge, so purchase toys with that in mind. There are many good, sturdy nylon toys available that will keep your puppy from teething on your bedroom slippers. These toys have the added benefit of messaging the gums and, consequently, will make the pup feel good, too. Various types of rawhide chews are also satisfactory.

Cords: Particularly dangerous are all electric cords that are accessible to the boxer. The dog could chew on them and receive a jolt of current that might prove fatal. You should also keep your telephone cord away from the dog.

Stairs: Slippery or open stairs or, even worse, stairs without railings should not be accessible to the puppy. It could fall.

Dangerous household objects: Put plastic bags, pieces of expanded plastics, and all sharp objects out of reach, because the puppy has a tendency to investigate everything and, if possible, to eat it.

Poisonous substances: Medications, of course, should never be stored where the dog can get at them. The same rule applies to household cleansers as well as to rat and mouse poisons.

Plants: Plants in your house and yard can be poisonous to your little four-legged friend. Someone at your local garden store will be glad to advise you about the plants you already own, and whenever you buy plants in the future, remember to ask about possible danger.

Traveling with Your Pet

For traveling with a young dog, the car is preferable to the train, because in a car you will have a chance to stop whenever necessary.

By car: Almost all dogs—including your boxer—enjoy riding in a car. To test your dog's "road fitness," you can make a short trial run. Before a relatively long car trip, do not feed your dog. It is a good idea to stop every two hours and take a short break to let the dog play and run a little and relieve itself. This is also a good time to give your pet fresh water. Do not feed it until you reach your destination.

Never leave your dog alone in the car in hot weather. Boxers suffer in high temperatures. Your pet might suffer a circulatory collapse that could prove fatal.

Abroad: When you travel abroad, observe the veterinary regulations in force in that country. You can learn what those are by asking your veterinarian or consulting the embassy of the country you plan to visit. In any event, a valid vaccination certificate is a necessity (see page 16). If you plan to take your boxer aboard an aircraft with you, ask the airline where you can get an approved airline pet carrier. The airlines will be glad to supply you with one for a charge. Have your veterinarian give your boxer a physical and provide you with a health certificate, which is now a mandatory requirement on all airlines. Be early for all flights and insist on seeing your pet loaded onto the airplane. Discuss the use of canine tranquilizers with your veterinarian and the advisability of your dog making this trip. Very old and very young dogs might be better left at home or in a boarding kennel.

The right way to put on the choke collar: The movable part of the chain should face toward the hand controlling the leash.

Getting the Puppy Settled

Everyone who buys a puppy longs feverishly for the day when the new housemate finally can be picked up and brought home. For the puppy, too, this day is an event of far-reaching significance in its young life: It will be separated from its mother and its littermates. Because it is being wrenched from its familiar environment, it naturally will be feeling very insecure in its new owner's company.

Transporting Your Pet

For the preceding reasons, you should not go alone to pick up your puppy, because it cannot be left unattended, especially in your car. The best time is morning. Then the puppy still has time to gain some familiarity with its new surroundings and family before its first night alone.

Before the trip: Ask the breeder not to give the puppy anything to eat during the hours just before you pick it up. The excitement could cause vomiting and diarrhea in the young puppy.

During the trip, puppies behave in a wide variety of ways:
• Some puppies may seek physical contact with their new owner and try to climb into his or her lap. On short trips, that is no problem at all; on longer trips, you can put the puppy on a blanket or a large towel placed on the floor in front of the passenger seat. Then, of course, you have to flip the air vents upward or close them completely.
• Other puppies feel no need for such closeness and are contented with a place by themselves. Under no circum-stances should the puppy be left alone on the backseat, however, because it could fall to the floor and become injured if you have to brake suddenly.

After the trip and a rest period lasting about one hour, the puppy should be given something to eat. If it is tired then, show it to its daytime sleeping spot. In its designated spot, you can place an old piece of clothing that you have worn, so that it can detect a familiar odor. The puppy also will cuddle right up with the clothing and thus feel somewhat less lonely.

The First Days and Nights

The first night is the worst, for both you and your puppy. It is during the first night that the little boxer will most miss its littermates. It feels lonely, is often very restless, and whimpers. Don't make the mistake of taking it into your bed. Certainly it will feel happier there because it is close to you, but it will consider your bed its nighttime sleeping place from then on—and that will not be so comfortable for you, particularly once your pet is fully grown. For these reasons, you need to place your dog's designated bed in a spot where it can see you and possibly smell you—at the end of your bed, for example. That will also be the easiest way for you to know when the boxer needs to go out at night, which is definitely a possibility during the early stages.

The adjustment phase: There is no general rule for predicting your puppy's behavior during the first few days and nights. Basically, the following applies:

Boxers are very receptive to teaching. All you have to do is to encourage their desire to learn from the outset.

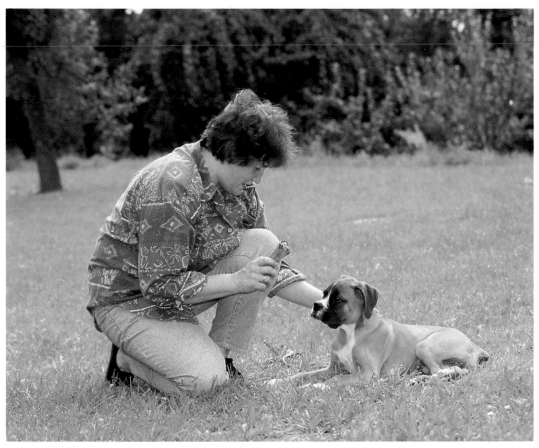

When a treat is being offered as a reward, the boxer has to obey your "down."

Observe your dog and learn to understand it. Give it ample time and opportunity to become accustomed to its new home in peace and quiet. Hectic movements and loud yelling can intimidate the puppy in its new environment. Another guideline: During the initial phase, don't show off your new pet to friends and relatives.

Lifting the puppy: If you want to pick up your puppy, there is only one way to go about it (see drawing, page 22): From behind, place one hand beneath its chest in such a way that all your fingers rest between its forelegs. Support its hindquarters with your other hand.

When you hold the puppy in your arms, make sure that its forelegs are close to its body and do not get bent, for example.

Caution: Never forget to hold the puppy securely. It may seem as still as can be—and then suddenly try to jump out of your arms. For the same reason, also use caution when children want to hold the puppy.

When you lift the puppy, always use one hand to support its hindquarters.

A Puppy Isn't Too Young to Learn

A puppy has to learn three lessons right at the outset: it has to become accustomed to the leash (see HOW-TO: Basic Training, page 30), answer to its name, and become housebroken.

Answering to its name: Many breeders give you an opportunity to choose a name for your boxer. Then the breeder can start early to call the puppy by its name. For you, that has an advantage: In most cases, your puppy already will answer to its name when it comes to your household.

Say your dog's name in a friendly, cheerful voice, never in connection with expressing your disapproval. When the dog obeys, praise it, give it a "treat" as a reward, or both.

Becoming housebroken: House-breaking your puppy requires some-what more effort. Always keep in mind that a housebroken puppy is more a result of your watchfulness and perse-verance than of the puppy's tractability.

• For these reasons, it is necessary to take the dog outdoors after every nap and meal.

• In the morning too, the puppy has to go out as soon as it wakes up. Wait until afterward for a good morning greeting; otherwise, your pet might have an accident.

• Select a place where your dog can relieve itself, and always take it to the same spot. That will help your pet con-nect the site with the activity more quickly.

• If the puppy was able to wait and succeeded in relieving itself outside, shower it with praise or give it a little treat. That way, "going outside" will always be a pleasant experience for it.

• If you keep a close eye on your puppy, you will quickly be able to tell when it has to go. In most cases, it will sniff extensively and turn around in circles. Some puppies also begin to scratch at the door after a short time, or stand at the door whimpering and barking to show that they need to go out.

• If a little accident should occur in your home—despite all your vigilance—it will be necessary to quickly and thor-oughly clean the spot with a disinfec-tant. Otherwise, the dog will keep on using that spot. In addition, scold your pet with a vigorous "Phooey" or "Bad dog." In the initial phase, a puppy may make 10 to 20 puddles a day, and you will have to get out of bed several times a night.

Note: The old method of rubbing the puppy's nose in its "business" is both absurd and ineffective.

Nap Time

A young dog also has to learn that it cannot race around and play all the time; it also needs many hours of sleep each day. There are some puppies that are so full of go that they have to be "forced" to sleep. To coax such a puppy to come to its bed, offer it a little snack and use a calm tone of voice. If necessary, sit down beside your pet for a little while. As a general rule, a puppy is so tired after playing that it will fall asleep.

My tip: If your boxer will not nap of its own accord, do not shut it up alone in a room. It will be miserable, whimper, and be completely unable to calm down. Rather, it has to learn that it can go to sleep with an easy mind and still find its family there when it wakes up. Once your boxer has developed this trust, it will sleep undisturbed even by the many background noises of your household, including the television, radio, and dishwasher.

The Boxer's Bed: Its Private Domain

Your dog should associate only positive things with its bed. For that reason you should allow your pet to bring its toys or bones to chew into its bed. Activities such as correcting your pet, giving it medications, and taking its temperature ought to be taboo there. Children also should respect the dog's special place. They need to learn that it belongs exclusively to their four-legged friend and that the boxer should not be disturbed there.

With Other Dogs

Teaching your pet proper social behavior toward other dogs is of great importance. A puppy can easily become accustomed to associating with other dogs. On the daily walk there will always be ample opportunity to let the puppy play with other dogs. An adult dog in most cases will accept the puppy and play with it.

Make sure the game doesn't get too rough; the puppy might be frightened or even injured. A single negative experience with other dogs can affect its patterns of social behavior. Ask the owners of the other dogs whether their pets are used to associating with puppies. If they are, there is no objection to their playing together. If your puppy has a chance to gain experience in dealing with other dogs, it will have no problems later, as an adult, in associating with other members of its species. Regardless of that, however, you will also find out that dogs, too, have their likes and dislikes.

Being Alone

If you are to avoid having to make extensive changes in your life on account of your new pet—such as giving up going out to dinner or to the movies—then your little four-legged friend has to learn to stay alone on occasion. You cannot leave it alone for hours at a time, however; even a fully grown boxer should not be left on its own for more than six hours. As soon as your puppy has settled into your home and is familiar with its new surroundings, you can safely try leaving it alone for ten minutes. Gradually you can increase that length of time. It is important for your little four-legged friend to learn that you will always come back.

Understanding Boxers

Not only can boxers communicate with other dogs, they also can make their emotions and wishes known to humans. Often enough you will intuitively give the correct interpretation to these signals. Alternatively, you can learn over time to interpret them by observing your pet closely.

Body Language

Boxers have a very special way of making themselves understood through body language and mimicry.

Alertness: If an unfamiliar noise, for example, catches your boxer's interest, it will hold its head at an angle and wrinkle its forehead.

Joy: Boxers, like other dogs as well, express pleasure by wagging their tail.

Contentment: On walks you surely will see time and again how your boxer, full of delight, throws itself down on the grass and rolls back and forth. It is brimming with exuberance. This behavior is a sign of its well-being. If it feels particularly good, it will lie on its side, totally relaxed. Lying on its back is an expression of absolute intimacy.

Submissiveness: Lying on its back, the boxer also presents its throat. That is a gesture of submissiveness. You will see it repeatedly during fights over rank order as well. The weaker dog lies on its back and presents its throat to the other dog. In this way it demonstrates that it is the underdog. The stronger dog's impulse to bite at it, however, is inhibited by its behavioral makeup. And, after all, the purpose of the dispute—to determine who is top dog—has been fulfilled.

When the boxer is feeling contented, it has a cocky, eager way of looking at you.

Sadness: If your boxer is sad, it will curl up in a ball. If you have punished your pet, it may be quite offended. Some boxers will turn away and fail to react even to treats or kind words.

Fear: A boxer shows fear by putting its tail between its legs. It reacts with the very same behavior when it has done something naughty and you then call it to come. Its head drooping and its tail tucked between its legs, it slinks toward you.

Expressive eyes: The boxer's eyes often express its feelings. To interpret these feelings correctly, however, you need to have known your pet for some time: its pleading look when it wants to get hold of a treat; its look of impatience when the daily walk is long overdue; then the happy look in its eyes when your boxer knows it is being allowed to come along.

Vocalization

The boxer has available a wide range of barks and other sounds with which it can express its state of mind and its wishes. It is not without good reason that all these utterances are described as vocalization. The more time you spend with your boxer, the more nuances the dog will express in its communication—and, conversely, the better you will understand your pet.

Whimpering and whining: The boxer indicates that it is in pain by means of high-pitched tones, produced with its mouth closed. When begging, too, it makes the same sounds—for example, when it wants something to eat or would like to go out.

When two dogs greet each other, they adhere to a precisely fixed pattern.

Growling: When the growling seems more like humming, it is an indication of your boxer's well-being; but if it is a deep rumble, the boxer is in a hostile mood and ready for a fight. Deep growling warns the opponent of the impending attack.

Barking: Where barking is concerned, both the timbre and the intervals between barks have information to convey. Even barking in a deep pitch is a sign of greeting, meant in a friendly way. Dislike is expressed by high-pitched, hectic barking.

Governed by Its Instincts

The boxer's behavior, like that of every other animal, is determined to a great extent by instinctive reactions and drives. In the final analysis, they serve the purpose of self-preservation or preservation of the species.

The instinct to resist enables the dog to defend itself.

The hunting or preying instinct expresses itself when the boxer chases an animal that is moving away from it and that it therefore views as a quarry.

Often this is only a kind of game of tag—for instance, when the boxer chases a hare. This pattern of behavior is enacted even though the boxer is not exactly a hunting dog. The boxer's training has to be aimed at repressing this drive as much as possible. Any impulses in this direction should be put to an end while still in their initial stages—for example, when your boxer digs in mouse nests or molehills. Similarly, do not let your pet chase deer and other game. To rule out the possibility of your dog being injured, you should consider whether you want to let your pet off its leash in an unenclosed hunting ground.

My tip: However obedient your boxer may be, you still have to expect that someday it will run after a wild animal in flight. When that happens, do not budge from the spot where your pet ran away from you. Do not run after it. Your boxer will get its bearings by means of its good sense of smell and will find its way back to you.

The instinct to protect applies not only to the boxer's offspring, but to its human family as well. On walks it will always check to make sure that its human pack is all accounted for. It grants its protection to children in particular. If you encounter other people with dogs, your boxer will become extremely alert. It will plant itself in front of you and bristle its hair. Once the "danger"—that is, the other dog— is past, its level of tension will decrease once more.

The instinct to look after and take care of others concerns primarily the puppies, but it can also extend to the littlest members of your family. It is expressed when the dog licks you— especially your face. For reasons of hygiene, you should not allow it to do so, because the boxer easily could transmit diseases or worms to you in this way. For this reason, try especially hard to keep the dog from licking your children, offer the boxer your ear or hands as an alternative.

The instinct to eat serves only one purpose: self-preservation. Nothing is altered by the fact that the boxer, as a house pet, no longer has to find food for itself, but is fed by its owner.

The mating instinct also has only one purpose: preservation of the species. It cannot be influenced by training.

To indicate complete subjugation, the boxer that loses the battle over rank order presents its throat to the winner.

Training: The Gentle Approach

Developmental Phases

To train your boxer correctly, you first need to learn something about the process of its development. It occurs in several different phases, each of which is linked to a certain age:

• vegetative phase: the first and second weeks of life
• transitional phase: the third week
• imprinting phase: the fourth through seventh weeks
• socialization phase: the eighth through twelfth weeks

In the imprinting phase the puppy's experiences become firmly fixed in its memory. What the puppy learns during this time it will retain all its life. However, what it does not learn it can never make up later on.

In the socialization phase, the dog integrates itself into its environment. Therefore the actual training process can take place during this period of time. That is why breeders let the puppies go to their new homes once they are eight weeks old.

Basic Obedience

In any event your boxer needs a basic level of obedience: It has to know the position assigned to it and behave accordingly.

The family as pack: Because the dog is a pack animal, it interprets its human family also, along with any other pets, as its pack. Within this human/dog pack your boxer also will instinctively keep trying to climb one rung higher in the hierarchy until it reaches the position of leader. That is reflected, for example, in its attempts to lie on the couch, armchair, or your bed. This is its way of striving to put itself on an equal footing with you. You cannot allow that to happen.

The human as pack leader: One member of the family has to lead the pack. In a dog pack there is always a single leader, and in your human/dog pack you have to take that position. Your boxer will accept that fact, too, if you get it used to playing a subordinate role from the outset. In the various situations that arise, you will see that the boxer is actually glad when it repeatedly receives confirmation of the position assigned it within the family. All you have to do is to lead it consistently and firmly toward acceptance of that position.

Consistency Is the Foundation

Your puppy's training begins at the very moment it comes in the door. That is when its acclimation to the human/dog pack starts. The goal of this process is for your boxer to take its place in the family rather than to dominate the family.

Laying down the rules: You and your family need to agree in advance on what the puppy is allowed to do and what is absolutely against the rules.

Include your children in these discussions, too, because consistency in enforcing the rules is the only way for your puppy to fit in successfully. For example, all the family members must present a united front in refusing to give the dog table scraps. Give it a treat from your plate once or twice—and the boxer will be perpetually begging whenever your family is at the table.

Abiding by the rules: Even if your puppy gives you a look of devotion, don't give in. Just the contrary: whenever your boxer begs at the table, a sharply uttered "Phooey" is appropriate. Even though that may seem harsh to you, you have to admit that a dog sitting beside the table and drooling is not exactly a pretty sight.

Receptiveness to Learning

The boxer is not exclusively governed by its instincts and drives. Otherwise, it would be unable to react appropriately to its environment. Its ability to learn puts it in a position to adjust to new situations. It learns by making associations between frequently recurring events and its own experiences during those events, and by firmly anchoring them in its memory. That is why you have to systematically practice a behavior that you want your pet to adopt. Over time, you can teach your boxer to obey certain commands.

However, the boxer also learns by observing, as described above. Its excellent powers of observation help it to correctly evaluate recurring situations. If, for example, its owner habitually puts on a coat and shoes before taking the boxer outdoors, it will eventually learn that a walk is in the offing. If the owner also takes the leash off the hook, the dog knows at once that the moment is at hand—and that it can come along.

Praise and Scolding

Rewards: With all training exercises, there is always a need for praise or, even better, a little treat in addition as a reward. In this way your boxer will connect the action you want it to perform with a pleasurable consequence for itself—and in time your pet will automatically perform as asked.

If you lavish your little four-legged friend with praise for everything it does correctly, you will achieve the greatest success in the quickest possible way.

Punishment: Whenever your boxer has failed to comply with one of the established rules, however, you have to punish it. In doing so, keep two things in mind:
• Your puppy will understand the admonition only if it immediately follows the transgression. Therefore, punish your puppy only when you catch it red-handed. Then it can draw some connection between its "misdeed" and the unpleasant aftermath.
• In addition, try to punish your boxer as a mother dog does her puppy: by shaking it (see HOW-TO: Basic Training, page 30).

Human speech. The best way to express criticism or praise is to talk quite normally with your boxer! Even though it cannot understand the majority of what you say, your intonation and the way you speak give the dog the message you would like to deliver. Words lovingly spoken tell the boxer that it has done something right. Harshly uttered words, such as "Phooey" or "No," give the dog the signal that you are dissatisfied with it. Don't be disappointed, however, if the dog doesn't immediately react the way you wish. Only with a great deal of patience can you help your boxer become ready and willing to learn the correct behavior.

P raise your boxer lavishly when it has done something especially well, but correct it immediately when it has been up to some "mischief"— that is the best way for the lesson to sink in.

Through its master's gestures and tone of voice, the boxer grasps what it is being asked to do.

HOW-TO:
Basic Training

Leash Training
Drawing 1

Your boxer also has to learn to walk on a leash, or a lead. It should move along at your side, keeping pace with you, without pulling on the leash. As a rule, it is not difficult to accustom a puppy to its collar and leash. To familiarize your puppy with its collar, put it on the boxer several times a day, for a brief period each time. Praise the dog while it is wearing the collar. In addition, play with your pet to divert it and help it overcome its uneasiness more quickly. After a short time, the collar will cease to bother it.

Next, attach the leash to the collar and take your boxer for a walk. Hold the leash in your left hand, and have the boxer walk at your left as well. Only when next to a bicycle should the dog walk

on the right, for reasons of safety. Make walking on the leash as pleasant as possible for your boxer: Praise it or give it a little treat; every young dog is susceptible to that kind of "bribery."

My tip: Never drag the puppy along behind you on its leash if it resists. Especially if that is a frequent occurrence, the dog will associate this negative experience with the leash and consequently try again and again to get the leash off.

Biting on the leash: On your daily walk, make sure that your boxer is not biting on its leash. That can lead to the loss of a tooth and, in addition, this practice is a disadvantage in the show ring (see Showing Your Boxer, page 59). Moreover, the leash is not a toy on which your boxer can pull and tug according to its fancy. Certainly it looks comical when the puppy strains against the leash with all its might, but keep in mind that one day it will be bigger and therefore stronger. Then it will cease to be a game: your pet will be taking you for a walk, instead of the other way around.

The "Sit" Command
Drawing 2

The boxer should respond to the "sit" command by sitting down on its hindquarters. Your dog has to perform this obedience exercise whenever you want to put on its leash, give it a treat, or prepare to cross a street with it. Start the lesson in the context of giving the boxer a treat. Do not let your pet have the treat until it is sitting down. You will

see that the boxer carries out the command very quickly when there is the prospect of a reward. If your pet does not sit down right away, help things along by gently pressing down on its rump.

The "Down" Command
Drawing 3

Whereas sitting on command should be performed only for short spans of time, the "down" position is intended for longer periods. Your boxer should assume this position when you leave it alone briefly or when you are seated at the dinner table.

Upon hearing the command "Down," the dog should lie down so that its hind legs are bent and its forelegs are stretched straight out. A puppy is still too young to be taught this obedience exercise. As a young dog—by the age of six months at the latest—the boxer can master it, however.

When teaching this lesson, you have to expect that your boxer will balk at first. Then you can

1) On a leash, the dog walks at its companion's left, at the same pace, without tugging at the leash.

2) To reinforce the "sit" command, gently press the dog's rear toward the ground.

3) When it hears the "down" command, the boxer should assume this position.

Correction
Drawing 4

If your boxer has been up to some mischief, you should punish your pet. Important here is prompt correction that directly follows the misdeed (see Praise and Scolding, page 28). Best of all, punish your pet the same way a dog would. Mother dogs take their puppies by the nape and give them a shake. Your puppy, therefore, is familiar with this type of punishment. Putting your hand on your boxer's nape, take its coat between your thumb and forefinger and shake the puppy a few times. For emphasis, you can also say "Phooey" or "Bad dog" and give your dog a talking-to in a scolding tone of voice.

simply help matters along a bit: as you call out "Down," tug the leash toward the ground without exerting force. And of course the same rule applies here as with all the other exercises: Every successfully executed command is to be followed by a reward.

Breaking Bad Habits

Jumping up: Jumping up on people, which is typical of boxers, is an annoying problem. Bubbling over with joy and high spirits, boxers love to jump up in order to get closer to their loved ones. You have to make it clear to your pet that it can be just as full of enthusiasm on all fours. If it jumps up on you, push it down and pat it when it has all four feet on the ground. Lend added emphasis with the words "Good dog, stay down" or "Don't jump up." Further, ask all family members and friends to follow exactly the same procedures. Once your boxer has formed the habit of jumping up, you will have trouble getting it to unlearn such behavior. Nevertheless, it is advisable that you do so. Your

boxer might one day jump up on a passerby, and that could lead to difficulties and prove costly as well.

Damaging the furnishings: Your boxer has to learn that it is not allowed to scratch at doors, chew on furniture, and bite rugs and other objects to pieces. If you catch your pet working away at a table leg with relish, give it a shake (see Correction, below) and back that up with a sharp "Phooey" or "Bad dog." To keep the boxer from temptation, give it toys to occupy it.

4) To scold the puppy for some misbehavior, hold it firmly by the nape and shake it.

Boxers Need to Be Busy

Every dog needs meaningful activity to keep from feeling unneeded and becoming dull and sluggish. If it is not kept occupied, your pet might possibly take out its surplus energy and boredom on your furniture. By virtue of its stamina and temperament, the boxer is suited for a great many activities.

Keeping Your Boxer Fit and in a Good Mood

Playing with children is always a pleasure for a boxer; children are its favorite playmates. A puppy—and, later on, the fully grown dog—automatically feels drawn to them. With children it can have a marvelous time romping, having races, and playing ball. A boxer that is accustomed early on to associating with children and has no negative experiences with them will enjoy playing with them all its life.

My tip: You will see how gently the dog treats the little children and how well it recognizes the difference between adults and children. Nevertheless, do not allow small chil-

Boxers never tire of retrieving a wooden dumbbell.

dren to go for a walk alone with a fully grown boxer.

Playing with other dogs provides two types of training for your boxer. First, your dog has a chance to let off steam; second, such encounters foster social contact (see With Other Dogs, page 23).

You can ride a bike with a boxer as your companion as soon as your pet is fully grown. Its stamina and willingness to run make the boxer an ideal partner on bicycle excursions.

Of course, you have to slowly introduce the dog to this type of activity. Start with just under 2 miles (3 km) and gradually increase the distance covered to 6 miles (10 km).

Does jogging appeal to you? Then go jogging with your boxer! Its physical endurance may turn out to offer you an incentive. In any event, your pet will thoroughly enjoy running along beside you. Incidentally, the type of sport you engage in is basically irrelevant, because only one thing matters to your dog— being with you.

Swimming is fun for some boxers. They are by no means tireless swimmers, but in hot summer weather they enjoy a cool dip from time to time. They especially like swimming with their master or mistress.

Guarding: If you have a front or back yard, you will get to see your boxer in the role of guard dog. True, it will simply lie there and observe things, but while doing so its mind is completely on its work, and the boxer is in its proper element. Incidentally, the boxer is not a yapper and will not bark at everyone out on the street who passes by its territory. But anyone who walks by property guarded by a boxer had better think twice before entering the premises unannounced.

Exercises such as drilling the "sit" command or throwing a stick to be

Specialized training programs at the dog training site take into account the boxer's ability.

fetched should always be made a part of the daily walk.

Agility and Specialized Training in a Dog Club

If you make a concerted effort to drill exercises with your dog and are interested in learning about additional types of activities, you can contact a dog club. For the address of a boxer training site near you, contact the American Boxer Club (see Useful Addresses and Literature, page 60).

Agility training with a partner: Many dog clubs now offer agility. In this type of dog sport, owner and dog together perform certain exercises, sometimes also in competition with other boxers and their owners (see HOW-TO: Specialized Training, page 34). To create the necessary partner relationship, there must be absolute trust between dog and owner.

Specialized training—schooling your pet's body and character. At the dog training site you also can train your boxer as a companion dog or a guard dog (see HOW-TO: Specialized Training, page 34). To do so, however, you must be a member of a club. In addition, your boxer has to be at least one year old. The programs include certain set exercises, all of which foster the boxer's willingness to subordinate itself. They are conducted in a group, under the guidance of an experienced teacher-trainer.

If training your boxer as a utility dog is not enough for you and you want to take part in athletic activities yourself, it is possible to participate in agility as a member of a dog sport club (see Useful Addresses and Literature, page 60).

Agility

Agility originated in England. It refers to a fitness program in which a dog and its owner together negotiate a course filled with obstacles of many different types, drawn from the various areas of dog sports as well as from equestrian sport. The boxer and its owner have to complete the course within a given time, without making any mistakes in negotiating the obstacles.

This type of dog sport presupposes absolute soundness of character as well as obedience on the part of the boxer, because in all the exercises and in the competition too, the boxer runs together with its owner and wears neither a leash nor a collar.

Obstacles on the Course
Drawing 1

The obstacles to be negotiated as part of agility include, for example, balancing on wooden planks, running through a slalom course, and crawling through a tunnel.

Negotiating a sloping wall: Among the most common obstacles to be overcome is the sloping wall. Here the boxer has to climb a slanting ramp on its own and come down the other side again (see Drawing 1). Meanwhile, its owner, keeping pace with the dog, runs alongside the obstacle. If the boxer is crossing over this obstacle for the first time, it is best to lead it on its leash. The second time, however, it should manage the obstacle on its own, without being leashed.

Specialized Training

If you think that your boxer needs, in addition to its basic training, a specialized or advanced type of training, you should take it to a dog training site.

1) Put your boxer on its leash the first time it goes over the sloping wall.

The tests: There are several tests that your boxer can take there. Possibilities are:
• Breeding suitability test: In Germany and various other European countries it is a requirement for obtaining approval to breed. In this test, the boxer's character traits are examined. It is valid, however, only if the following test is also passed:
• Stamina test: The dog's handler has to ride a distance of 12 miles (20 km) on a bicycle, with the boxer trotting alongside on its leash.
• Tracking dog test.
• Companion dog test.
• Guard dog tests.

The Companion Dog Test
Drawings 2 and 3

Every dog handler who works regularly with his or her boxer should have the companion dog test as a goal. To pass it, the boxer has to furnish proof of leash training, master the "sit"

2) The boxer is not supposed to jump up when it loses visual contact with its owner.

and "down" exercises (see HOW-TO: Basic Training, page 30), and be able to follow at "heel" off-lead.

"Long down" while being distracted: This exercise, also a component of the companion dog test, refers to assuming the "down" position and

3) The dog has to remain lying down, even when its owner goes away and another dog is nearby.

maintaining it while the boxer's owner walks away and, at the same time, another owner walks past with his or her boxer (see Drawing 3).

"Long down" while the owner goes out of sight: In this exercise, the dog takes the "down" position while its owner walks away and disappears behind a screen (see Drawing 2). Here, too, the boxer is required to maintain its position unswervingly, even when it no longer sees its owner.

An additional part of the test takes place away from the dog training site. Here the boxer has to show that it can also move about in city traffic as the situation demands.

The Guard Dog Tests
Drawing 4

The guard dog tests could be subdivided into three individual tests: 1, 2, and 3. To participate, the dog must have passed the companion dog test and must be at least 18 months old. Each of the three tests includes the following:

Tracking work: In this portion of the test, the boxer has to fur-

nish proof that it is able to clearly identify trails that are as much as three hours old.

Subordination: In addition to the skills required in the companion dog test, this category includes exercises of greater difficulty, such as clearing a hurdle just over 3 feet (1 m) high, with and without a wooden dumbbell stick carried in the boxer's mouth; and negotiating a sloping wall about 5 feet 11 inches (1.8 m) high.

Acting as a guard: Here the boxer learns to protect its owner when attacked by another person. It has to bark at the attacker and keep him at bay without physically assaulting him.

Retrieving also is part of the standard program of the guard dog tests. In this exercise, the boxer brings back to its owner a wooden dumbbell that the owner has thrown (Drawing 4). At the beginning of the exercise, the boxer has to assume the "sit" position beside its owner. Then the owner tosses the wooden dumbbell into the distance. Once it hits the ground, the boxer can rush off and retrieve it. Finally, it has to lay the dumbbell down at its owner's feet.

4) The boxer has to sit still while the wooden dumbbell is being thrown. Once it hits the ground, the dog can race off and retrieve it.

35

Presenting its abdomen is a great sign of trust.

The Daily Routine and New Experiences

Keeping to the "schedule": With all the activities that you undertake in order to keep your boxer occupied, it is important that they take place on a regular basis. Your pet will get used to a regular daily routine. Soon it will know when it is time to be fed and when it is time for its walk. It will then wait for these events to occur.

Trying out unfamiliar situations: It is equally important to introduce your boxer to a wide variety of situations. It will learn from them and in this way develop the desired strength of character. A dog that is afraid of everything can quickly become a dog that bites when scared.

If you live in the country, just take your boxer along into town sometime. It will adjust quite well to this new situation and learn to deal with the noise, the cars, and the crowds of people.

Daily Grooming and Health Check

Your boxer needs a daily grooming routine. Get it accustomed to this process while still a puppy. Quite likely, however, your pet will already have become familiar with such procedures at the breeder's, where it was weighed and kept clean daily. In any event, it is very important that your dog submit to all the grooming procedures you institute. That includes allowing you to put your hand in its mouth, because you have to be able at all times to take something out of the boxer's mouth. You also have to be able to give the dog tablets or drops (see HOW-TO: Health, page 54).

The boxer's daily grooming includes the care of its coat, eyes, ears, and nails. This daily ritual is intended primarily to keep the boxer healthy and content, but it simultaneously promotes contact with the dog's "significant human."

Routine Examination

Additionally, a periodic check to detect signs of possible disease can be linked with daily hygienic measures: Owners who spend a great deal of time with their pet will be able to tell whether the dog really feels well. Especially while performing the various steps of the daily grooming routine, you have an excellent opportunity to check specifically for indications of health problems. It is best to go through the following checklist each time:
• Are the boxer's eyes clear and clean, or is a sticky discharge present? Do its eyes tear? Are they reddened?
• Are its ears free of parasites?
• Is its coat glossy and close fitting? Is it dull? Is it bare in patches?
• Is the dog listless or sluggish?

Fleas and Other Parasites

Parasites are organisms that receive nutriment from the bodies of other living creatures. Among the animals they infest are boxers. If you find parasites on your boxer, you need to treat it immediately.

Worms can cause vomiting, diarrhea, and weight loss. In puppies, they also lead to disturbances of growth. An unmistakable sign of worm infestation in a puppy is an overly distended abdomen. A worm infestation is most likely to be detected in the stool. There you can see the little white eggs or even the worms themselves.

Treatment: Initiate veterinary treatment immediately.

My tip: Depending on the species, worms are transmitted not only via foodstuffs but above all through sniffing at other dogs' droppings. Consequently, you need to keep your boxer from developing that habit.

Fleas: Fleas feed on a dog by biting it and sucking its blood. Their bites often cause severe itching and, above all, skin infections. Open sores resulting from the dog's biting and scratching are an ideal breeding ground for pathogens. Because fleas migrate

HOW-TO:
Grooming

The grooming of your boxer is not very time consuming, but it has to be performed regularly and meticulously.

Eye Check

The boxer's eyes have to be clear. The eyes of this breed in particular are somewhat sensitive. A draft—created when the dog rides in a car with the windows open, for example—may well result in conjunctivitis.

Conjunctivitis: The affected eye will begin to tear. The inflammation can be cured with an ophthalmic ointment.

"Open" eyes: Some boxers are afflicted with this condition, in which the lower eyelid droops slightly. That causes increased secretion of lachrymal fluid. Drafts may also be a contributing factor. A flow of tears ensues. If it becomes chronic, skin irritations and hair loss may occur in the muzzle area.

1) Clean the ears with a cloth dipped in oil.

If you detect these symptoms, have your pet's eyes examined by the veterinarian, who will prescribe special ointments. Before application, clean the dog's eyes very carefully with a damp cloth, making sure not to rub.

Cleaning the Ears
Drawing 1

The ears have to be checked regularly, and any wax and dirt particles need to be removed. Some boxers tend to secrete large amounts of wax, whereas others produce none at all.

To clean the ears, it is best to use a cloth soaked in oil. It is all right to use baby-care wipes for this purpose. Do not use cotton swabs to get deeper into the ear. They could easily injure the inner portion of the ear, which is extremely sensitive.

In any event, the boxer seldom gets dirt in its ear, which is quite short and floppy. Particularly with ears of this type, however, more frequent ear checks are necessary. Because air flow is relatively poor, inflammations arise more readily, and they have to be treated by a veterinarian.

Your boxer may also suffer from ear mites (see Fleas and Other Parasites, page 37). If so, it will constantly scratch and scrape at its ears. Take your pet to the veterinarian: only he or she can provide you with the proper medications to bring relief and healing.

Cleaning the Mouth
Drawing 2

The lips need to be cleaned after every meal, to prevent

2) After the dog eats, clean its mouth with a soft cloth.

food remnants from accumulating in the folds of the muzzle and possibly causing inflammation. For this reason, clean the folds thoroughly. Use a hand towel to wipe the area between the boxer's lips and its teeth. It is best to use clear water and soap that contains no fragrances.

This procedure will prevent your boxer from wiping its muzzle on your upholstered furniture and articles of clothing.

Cleaning the Feet

You need to check your pet's feet with some degree of frequency. Particularly after a walk in winter, that is essential. Otherwise, thawing salt, sand, and gravel will irritate the skin.

In addition, regular foot care should include checking between your pet's toes. If you fail to remove small pebbles and other dirt particles, small injuries to the balls of the toes can result, and they can become inflamed.

The nails should be clipped by the veterinarian, who has the ability to determine precisely where the quick lies and where the dead keratin begins. If your pet frequently runs on concrete, its nails usually get worn down on their own.

The balls of the feet need no special care, but in winter you can rub them with butterfat or deer tallow to keep them supple. Make sure not to use too much of these moisturizers. Otherwise, the balls of the feet will become too soft, and they could tear.

Coat Care
Drawings 3 and 4

Every few days, groom the boxer's coat with a so-called hound-glove, a rubber currycomb, a good brush, or a chamois cloth (see Drawing 3).
• With the rubber currycomb, brush the dog's coat the wrong

3) Tools for coat care: chamois, brush, rubber currycomb.

4) Using the rubber currycomb, vigorously brush the boxer's coat the wrong way.

way (see Drawing 4). Give it a good going-over. Most of the hairs that come off will stay in the currycomb.
• Use the brush to go over the coat once more.
• Finally, rub your boxer all over with the chamois or hound-glove.

Be sure to brush the dog's abdomen, neck, and inner thighs as well. The intense mechanical working over of the entire coat stimulates the circulation of the skin. As a result, the coat acquires a velvety gloss.

Replacement of the hair coat: Twice a year the boxer grows a new coat of hair. Unlike the German shepherd and rottweiler, for example, it lacks an undercoat to protect it from variations in temperature.

When you brush the boxer's coat the wrong way at the start of the cold season or the warm one, you will be amazed to see how many hairs are shed. At these times of year, brush your dog daily to spare yourself the job of constantly removing the hairs from furniture and clothing.

Bathing
When? Generally, you should bathe your boxer only when it is absolutely necessary—for example, when the dog is extremely dirty and has an unpleasant smell. You need to exhibit restraint because every bath affects the natural protective coating of the skin. Generally, because the boxer's coat is so short, a rubdown with a chamois (see Drawing 3) or a towel after every walk is sufficient.

How? When you bathe your boxer, use a mild shampoo for dogs. At the end of the bath, your pet has to be rinsed off thoroughly. Do not let the shampoo get in the dog's eyes, ears, and mouth, because it irritates the mucous membranes. As a final step, dry the dog well and keep it indoors for the next few hours, to keep it from catching cold.

Pointer: Do not bathe a puppy until after its first birthday. Remove any dirt with baby oil.

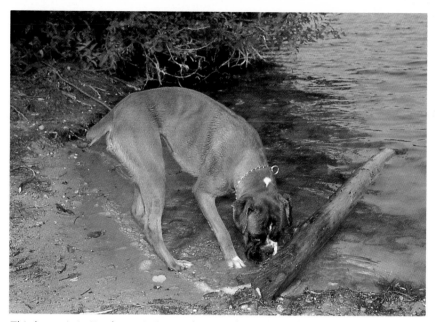

This boxer is in its element: Curiously, it explores the unknown . . .

from one dog to another, transmission of diseases also is within the realm of possibility. Fleas love warm weather, but they can appear independently of the season, in either summer or winter.

If your boxer scratches itself incessantly, it probably has fleas. You can conduct a flea inspection by carefully scrutinizing the dog's coat. Check it on a regular basis. Fleas are visible to the naked eye.

Treatment: Pet stores offer a variety of sprays and powders that you can apply to your pet. You can also get rid of fleas by giving the dog a warm bath with a specially formulated shampoo. In addition, you can put a flea collar on your boxer. Be careful, though: Some dogs are allergic to the collars.

My tip: Always include the dog's bed and the surrounding area when you treat the boxer with insecticidal

sprays. Fleas, along with their eggs, often settle in blankets and bedding.

Mites are most commonly found on the neck, ears, and eyes, but they also inhabit the area around the eyes. The external signs of mite infestation on your dog are frequent scratching, hair loss, and scaly skin.

Treatment: If you think your pet has mites, take it to the veterinarian. He or she will be able to tell what kind of mite is involved and initiate treatment. The presence of ear mites can cause a dark, dirty, waxy material to adhere to the inner skin of the ear. Ear mites can cause your pet a great deal of discomfort, as evidence by excessive ear scratching or violent head shaking. See your veterinarian immediately.

My tip: Before traveling abroad, find out what parasites might endanger your dog at your destination, and ask your veterinarian for the appropriate medications.

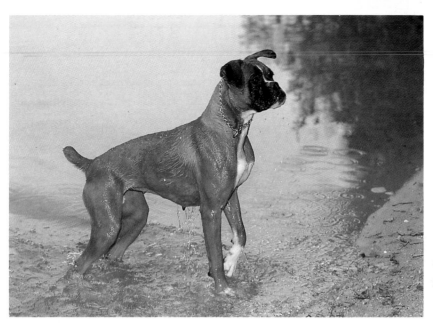

. . . and then takes a cool dip!

Ticks: These parasites usually appear in the spring. They lodge themselves firmly in the boxer's skin and suck themselves full of blood. As they do so, their original size increases fivefold. You need to examine your pet for ticks after every walk. Ticks like to get into a boxer's large ears. But don't confuse these with the much smaller ear mites.

Treatment: If you find a tick, remove it immediately by grasping the entire head and body and pulling it directly out of your pet's skin. Pet stores sell special tick tweezers that make such removal easy. When removing the tick, the most important thing is to make sure that the head comes out along with the body; otherwise, infection can result. Should that occur, take the dog to the veterinarian right away.

Lyme disease is a serious, potentially fatal disease that affects warm-blooded animals and humans. Because your boxer should walk and play in parks or other wooded areas, the possibility of exposure to Lyme disease must be considered. The ailment can even be contracted in your pet's own backyard.

Lyme disease, first identified in Lyme, Connecticut, is spread primarily by the deer tick, a tiny bloodsucker credited with carrying an illness that can do your boxer, and you, great physical harm! Borelliosis (the medical name of this disease) can affect your dog in several ways, but usually swelling and tenderness around the joints is observable.

If you have been bitten by a tick or see the telltale tick bite with its characteristic surrounding of red (somewhat like a bull's-eye on a target), consult your physician or county health department. Timely diagnosis and treatment are essential.

Proper Nutrition and Feeding

This chapter deals with the feeding and nutrition of fully grown dogs. You have already been given nutritional information for puppies (see Advantages of Buying from a Breeder, page 16). The feeding of a pregnant or lactating bitch is a special topic, which you can read about elsewhere (see Useful Addresses and Literature, page 60).

Commercial Dog Food

Commercial dog food is the easiest way to give your dog a balanced, appropriate diet. If you stick to the recommended daily amounts listed on the packaging, you can be certain that your boxer is getting all the necessary vitamins, minerals, trace elements, proteins, and other important supplements in the right quantities and proper ingredients.

Commercial dog food has yet another advantage. Most products of this kind can be served in either moist or dry form, and that makes them suitable for taking along on trips.

My tip: Especially during the summer months, it is a good idea to feed your pet dry food. That way you will keep odors from forming and attracting flies and other insects.

When Buying Dog Food

A great number of dog food products from various manufacturers are available commercially. Ideally, commercial dog food should contain:

• no flavor or fragrance enhancers; they lead the dog to develop an excessive appetite, which ultimately results in extra poundage that is detrimental to its health;
• no preservatives (antioxidants); they extend the perishability of the fat contained in the dog food, but they can cause allergic reactions;
• no coloring agents; they are meant more to appeal to the eye of the buyer—the boxer attaches no importance to brightly colored vegetable flakes.

Buy quality: Don't try to be thrifty. A well-prepared, nutritionally balanced commercial dog food comes at a price. If you buy a dog food of lower quality, your boxer might refuse to eat it. If your boxer is thriving, gaining weight, and not suffering from diarrhea, then you have found the right dog food.

Freshly Prepared Dog Food

It may be that your boxer does not enjoy commercial dog food as a steady diet. If your pet is a gourmet and wants something special in its bowl from time to time, you have no option but to feed it fresh food that you yourself prepare. That is not altogether easy, because:

• You need a source of supply. Not every butcher is willing to give you scraps from his shop.
• You have to add the required vitamins, trace elements, and minerals to the food in the right quantities and composition.

• The food has to be cooked or at least boiled in water or broth in order to kill any viruses present—but the smell may not be to everyone's liking.

Guidelines for Home-prepared Meals

Meat absolutely has to be bought with an eye to quality control. You can purchase fresh meat from a butcher or frozen meat in the larger pet stores. Frozen meat has the advantage of being packaged in serving-size amounts and already cut up. All you have to do is to thaw out a suitable portion, cook it or heat it in water or broth, and add the other ingredients. You can feed your pet beef, lamb, poultry, or venison.

Caution: Pork, if used at all, always should be cooked until completely done, but it is better not to feed your dog pork. It could contain the deadly trichina nematode, which causes trichinosis.

Fish also may be included in your dog's diet. It supplies protein of high nutritive value.

Dairy products: Farmer cheese and cottage cheese are also excellent additions to your boxer's feeding program. Cow's milk is a valuable food for dogs.

It is best to add a teaspoon of honey to the milk and serve it lukewarm.

Pointer: Use only low-fat milk, however; otherwise, it will cause diarrhea in your boxer.

Eggs: One egg yolk or one hard-boiled egg per week should also be included in your dog's meal plan.

Cereal products: Rice, barley, and noodles are well liked by boxers, and they round out the meal. Unhusked rice (paddy rice) can also be served when your dog is on a special diet, because it acts as a powerful dehydrant.

Vegetables are part of any balanced feeding program. Easy-to-use kinds include carrots, tomatoes, zucchini, fennel, cauliflower, and all leafy vegetables. Watercress may also be used, though only in small amounts. Legumes like peas, beans, and lentils are not suitable. Vegetables should be steamed briefly. Overcooking reduces the vitamin content.

Fruits: All kinds of fruits can be fed to your pet. With stone fruits, remember to remove the stone or pit. In winter, a few orange wedges each day will provide the requisite amount of vitamin C.

Fat and oil are also essential components of your boxer's nutritional plan.

The most important item in the boxer's diet is water. It always has to be fresh.

When the heat is really getting to you, panting is the only thing that helps.

Vegetable oils, which are higher in unsaturated fatty acids, are easier to digest. As little as 1 tablespoon of oil added to the dog's food each day will improve its coat. Sunflower oil or thistle oil are best for this purpose.

Vitamins: In any event, the meals you prepare have to be planned so as to give your boxer all the vitamins it needs, in sufficient quantities.

The following foods contain the essential vitamins in relatively high concentrations:
• Vitamin A: carrots, parsley, tomatoes, spinach, leafy vegetables, milk, fish, egg yolk, and butter
• Vitamin B: yeast, milk, liver, heart, leafy vegetables, eggs
• Vitamin C: citrus fruits, parsley, spinach, milk
• Vitamin D: cod-liver oil (add to your pet's food only in winter)

Seasonings

Iodized table salt is healthful in small quantities. The seasonings people love, however—pepper, paprika, and the like—are not good for their pets. Garlic, on the other hand, is recommended. It is not only healthful, but also acts as a safeguard against worms (see Fleas and Other Parasites, page 37). You need to feed it to your boxer regularly, however.

Bones and Treats

Bones of any kind are not suitable for boxers. True, with its powerful set of teeth, a boxer is easily able to utterly demolish bones. Bone splinters can cause life-threatening internal injuries, however. That is why all veterinarians are opposed to feeding bones to dogs.

Rawhide bones, available in every pet store, make a good substitute. They are suitable for dogs and easy to digest, and they also will keep your pet's teeth clean. Even a puppy can be given a rawhide bone to satisfy its urge to chew and to keep it amused.

Bread that has hardened is something that boxers dearly love to nibble on.

Dog biscuits do more than satisfy your dog's hunger. The large, coarse ones in particular serve as our pet boxer's toothbrush.

My tip: After the final meal of the day, go ahead and give your boxer one or two dog biscuits, but be sure to add these calories to the daily total.

Snacks are available in a wide assortment. Here, of course, your individual dog's taste plays a role. Naturally you will not give your dog chocolate of any kind. Pet stores offer a broad range of suitable products, and you can choose between sweet and savory tastes. You should not view these snacks as a substitute for food, however, but as true rewards.

Pointer: Keep in mind that treats mean extra calories, and they have to be counted as such if your dog is on a special diet.

Feeding Your Boxer

How often? Generally, an eight-week-old puppy still has to be fed four times a day. A fully grown dog, however, needs one feeding per day. It is preferable, however, to divide the daily ration into two meals. That way the dog does not ingest too much food at one time, and its stomach is not overloaded. Don't make the mistake of setting out the full bowl for your pet in the morning, so that it can help itself whenever it likes.

When? You can determine the feeding time in accordance with your daily routine. It is a good idea to feed your pet in the morning and in the evening. In any case, however, you need to stick to whatever feeding schedule you adopt.

Important: After you feed your boxer, it needs to rest for an hour, so that it can digest its meal.

For a Thirsty Dog

The most important item in your boxer's diet is water. Sometimes a dog can go without food for several days without any difficulties, but it can never get by without water. The danger that your pet would become dehydrated is enormous.

Always give your boxer fresh water. Don't just keep filling up its water bowl; clean the bowl thoroughly every day to keep bacteria from accumulating there.

Caution: Make sure that your boxer does not drink from bodies of standing water, including puddles. The stagnant water can contain coli bacteria, and disease can result.

Proper Nutrition for Young Dogs

The feeding of a puppy (animals up to six months in age) usually is up to

After meals, a nap is called for.

Important Rules for Feeding

1. Feed your boxer one or two times daily.

2. Always feed your pet at the same times of day.

3. Do not feed your dog by hand. Your boxer should have its own bowl.

4. The food should be at room temperature. Never give a dog food straight from the refrigerator.

5. Your boxer needs to have a good appetite. If it stands listlessly in front of its bowl and pokes around in the food or perhaps picks out certain items, take the bowl away. Although it may sound heartless, let the boxer go hungry—it will eat the next meal all the more readily.

6. With an adult boxer, it is even advisable to institute one fast day per week. Of course, you still have to give your pet fresh drinking water on its fast day.

7. Don't offer the dog any substitutes for its regular diet; you will produce a finicky pet. At each regular meal you will be wondering "Is the boxer going to eat or not?" Once you have offered your pet a substitute, which it may have found even tastier than its standard meal, you will have to keep resorting to special tidbits to induce the dog to eat.

8. Base the amount you serve on the dog's actual appetite. If your boxer doesn't finish its meal, the portion was too large; reduce it. If it keeps licking its bowl, however, it is perfectly all right to increase the amount.

9. Have your boxer rest for one hour after every meal.

---

the breeder initially, and it can vary widely. Ask your breeder what the puppy was fed up to the time it joined your family, and feed it exactly the same diet during its first weeks in your home (see Advantages of Buying from a Breeder, page 16). Pet stores now sell excellent products, specially formulated by the pet food industry, for rearing puppies and young dogs. Many breeders prefer them because they are nutritionally balanced. But whatever you feed your pet, the following rules apply:

• Food for puppies has to be high in protein.

• In addition, dogs need calcium in this early stage of life. It is important for their second set of teeth, which come in roughly by the end of the fourth month, and for bone formation, which occurs at this time.

Puppies should be fed four times a day.

A young dog (up to one year), however, needs food only three times a day. The makeup of the meals, however, should remain the same as that of the puppy's meals. Appropriate food mixes are available in pet stores.

Proper Nutrition for Old Dogs

When your boxer is getting on in years (older than six months), you need to make a change in its diet. Today many pet food manufacturers offer products specially formulated for puppies, adults, and food for "senior" dogs. These foods are lower in protein. If you don't want to use them—or to use them exclusively—then give your senior boxer farmer cheese with some frequency, as well as plenty of vegetables and fruit, but little meat.

Feed your pet several times a day. One meal per day places too much stress on aging organs.

If Your Boxer Is Too Fat

Why get rid of excess weight? Being overweight is detrimental to your boxer's health. In your pet as well, excess poundage is a civilizational disease. Too much food, including too many between-meal treats in particular, and too little exercise lead to serious weight gain in a boxer—and once the boxer is too fat, it is no longer able to get enough exercise. Inactivity, in turn, has a negative effect on the dog's organs, ligaments, tendons, and muscles.

Is my pet overweight? You can determine without a doubt whether your boxer is too fat. If its ribs are no longer discernible, it is carrying excess poundage. In a boxer of normal weight, however, you can clearly see the play of the ribs (see photo, page 53). From behind your pet, lay your hands on either side of its chest. You should be able to easily detect the path of the ribs when you press lightly on the boxer's chest. If you have to exert greater pressure to reach the ribs, your boxer is unmistakably too fat.

The size of your boxer, however, also has some bearing on your conclusion. A small representative of the breed, naturally, should not produce a reading of much more than 70 pounds (31.8 kg) on the scales, and a female need not necessarily weigh the same as a male (see The AKC Breed Standard, page 6).

How can my dog lose weight? To reduce the excess poundage effectively, the dog first has to shed some of its padding. Only then can you slowly start a long-term program of physical training. Rice is especially effective in reducing fat deposits, because it has a dehydrating effect and gives a feeling of fullness. So-called "light" products are among the commercial dog foods now available. They are also suited for weight reduction, because they fill up the dog's stomach but are lower in calories. Occasionally give the boxer a piece of fruit or vegetables. While your pet is on its weight-reduction diet, weigh it once a week. That is the only way to tell whether the diet is working and the dog is indeed losing weight.

Rawhide bones satisfy the dog's urge to chew and also keep its teeth clean. They are suitable even for puppies.

Preventive Health Care and Illnesses

To detect signs of possible illness, you need to be very familiar with your boxer and observe it closely.

There are a number of contagious diseases that your boxer easily can contract, and they can become life threatening. Vaccination offers effective protection against them.

Vaccinations

When you pick up your boxer puppy at the breeder's it usually has been vaccinated against distemper, measles, and hepatitis, and possibly, for parainfluenza, corona-virus, bordetella, and leptospirosis. This basic series of immunizations is recorded in a vaccination certificate, which the breeder is required to give you when you take possession of the puppy (see What the Buyer Needs to Know, page 14). In most instances, the puppy also will have been vaccinated against parvovirus disease. If that is not the case, you should have it done. It is also advisable to vaccinate the dog against kennel cough viruses.

Follow-up Vaccinations on Schedule

About four weeks after the first vaccination, the puppy has to be vaccinated again. Only then will it have adequate immunity to the diseases listed above. At least four weeks after that, have your boxer vaccinated against rabies as well.

If your pet is to have lifelong immunity to these dangerous infectious diseases, regular booster shots are necessary (see Vaccination Schedule, page 51). The vaccinations against leptospirosis, rabies, parvovirus disease, and kennel cough viruses have to be repeated on an annual basis. To keep immunity to distemper and hepatitis current, boosters every one or two years are usually sufficient.

My tip: If you have questions about special situations—for example, if you are planning to have your bitch bred—your veterinarian will be happy to help by providing appropriate advice. Also ask your veterinarian for information about the vaccine used to inoculate your boxer.

The vaccination certificate of your boxer records every inoculation given the dog (see What the Buyer Needs to Know, page 14). It also will serve as a reminder of the date the next shot is due. At dog shows and on trips abroad with your boxer, the vaccination certificate is an indispensable document.

Worming

No dog is safe from worm infestation, and these parasites can cause enormous health problems (see Fleas and Other Parasites, page 37). Therefore you need to check your dog for worms on a regular basis. Discuss with your veterinarian about administering three worm treatments after the first eight weeks of life. At least twice a year, bring a stool sample to your veterinarian (who will provide you with appropriate containers for that

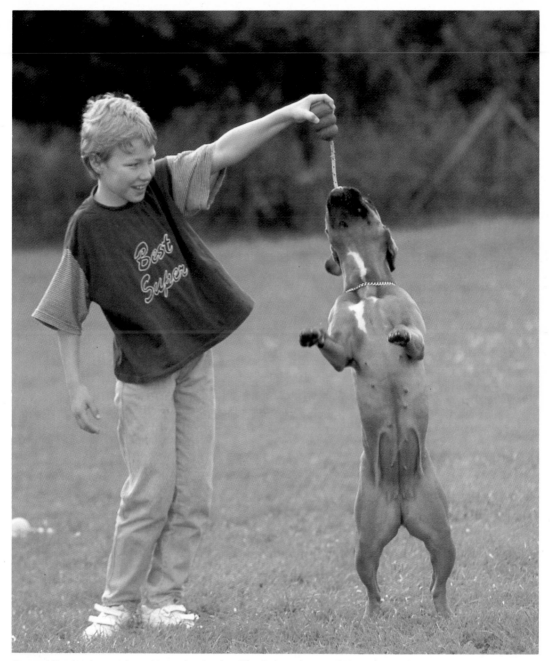

One of the best ways for a boxer to stay healthy is to get enough exercise.

purpose). If your pet is found to have worms, the veterinarian will prescribe the proper remedy.

Important: Preventive worming is not recommended, because it assaults the boxer's stomach and intestines unnecessarily.

How to Tell if Your Dog Is Ill

If you know your boxer well, you will quickly detect any deviations from its normal state of health and behavior. Certain symptoms are considered warning signs of possible disease:

• Is your boxer's nose dry?
• Does its coat show any changes?
• Does your pet suffer from lack of appetite?
• Does it exhibit continual fatigue?
• Does it deliberately creep away and hide?
• Is its behavior characterized by sluggishness and dullness?
• Is it ill-humored?
• Does it display, contrary to its nature, exaggerated fearfulness?

Boxers have great stamina when they run; if they give up quickly and are listless, they may be ill.

• Is it restless for no apparent reason?
• Does it whimper and howl strangely, for no obvious reason?

If one of these symptoms is present, there is no need to rush to the veterinarian's office. The cause of the unusual behavior may be entirely harmless. The dog's nose, for example, may be dry after digging in the ground, after sleeping, on very hot days, and even, at times, in a bitch in heat. In all of these cases, however, the nose will be cool and moist again a short time later.

My tip: First, keep a very close eye on your boxer if you detect any indications of a possible illness. Above all, take your pet's temperature. If the dog has fever or if one or more symptoms begin to worsen, it is time to visit the veterinarian.

When a Veterinarian's Help Is Essential

There are, however, some symptoms that call for an immediate trip to the veterinarian:

• Severe itching accompanied by intense scratching: This is excruciating for the dog, and it can have a variety of causes, all of which are serious, however.
• Weight loss in connection with greatly increased thirst and chronic eczema on the back: This usually results from a kidney disorder.

Gastric torsion: All large dog breeds, including boxers, can in isolated cases develop the dreaded gastric torsion (bloat) after eating. Accumulation of gas in the stomach, excessive amounts of food, or overly large pieces of food can cause the stomach to "tilt," twisting about 180 degrees. You can spot this problem by the dog's greatly distended abdomen and pronounced indisposition. In such a case, get your pet to the veterinarian posthaste.

When You Can Treat Your Pet Yourself

For constipation, add dry yeast to your boxer's food or conceal brewer's yeast in a little morsel of food. You might even give the dog some castor oil. Brewer's yeast stimulates the intestinal flora, and that quickly restores the dog's digestion to normal. It should never be mixed with the dog's food, however, because it can cause it to ferment. If no improvement is evident, it is best to take your pet to the veterinarian.

For diarrhea, withhold all food from your boxer for one day. Alternatively, give it a human anti-diarheal medicine that does not contain aspirin. If no improvement ensues, here, too, it is necessary to take your pet to the veterinarian.

Hip Dysplasia

Hip dysplasia (HD) is a typical disorder of medium-size and large dog breeds. Boxers too are susceptible to it. HD is a congenital defect of the hip joint, which—depending on the severity of the case—can lead to weakening or even paralysis of the hind legs. The symptoms are as follows:
- Rising from a sitting or lying position is painful for the boxer.
- Climbing stairs also causes it pain.
- Physical exertion causes it to tire quickly.
- Over relatively long distances, the boxer runs fast and hops.
- It has trouble jumping.

The condition can be definitely diagnosed only by an X ray, which can be taken once the dog has reached 12 months of age. Any pain and inflammation that may appear can be eased with medication prescribed by the veterinarian. For serious, persistent discomfort, surgical insertion of an artificial hip joint generally has good results. One preventive measure has proved valuable: Do not feed the growing dog too rich a diet.

Vaccination Schedule for Preventive Health Care

Serum to prevent:	Basic Series of Shots			Booster Shots
	Week 7 to 8	Follow-up shots Week 10 to 12	After about Week 12	12 Months After Basic Series
Parvovirus disease (live vaccine)	x	x		Annually
Distemper	x	x		Annually
Hepatitis	x	x		Annually
Leptospirosis	x	x		Annually
Rabies	x		x	Annually

Important: Vaccinations do not grant immunity instantaneously. It takes about one or two weeks for immunity to develop.

On Aging and Dying

You will see that your boxer alters with increasing age. Its exuberant temperament will become calmer, its step will grow slower, its vision and hearing will become weaker, and more and more gray hairs will appear—your dog is getting old. It will sleep a great deal and seek contact with you with mounting frequency. Go along with the changes in its needs, and be considerate of its infirmities. Your boxer requires your loving care now, and it has a great need for peace, quiet, and security.

The following health problems appear with great frequency in old boxers—and here's what you can do to alleviate them:
• Signs of wear and tear in joints and in the spinal column: always keep the boxer warmly covered; take shorter, but more frequent, walks.
• Cardiac and circulatory insufficiency: make sure your pet doesn't overdo things, and calm it down when excited.
• Bad teeth: give your boxer rawhide bones more often (see Bones and Treats, page 44) or clean its teeth with a toothbrush.

The dog's behavior reflects its state of mind.

Having the veterinarian put it to sleep. Sooner or later the day will come when you realize that your boxer is suffering from its infirmities and that there is no hope of remedying its painful condition. When that time arrives, you should decide to have your dog put to sleep. The veterinarian will give your boxer an injection containing an overdose of a tranquilizer, and that will ensure your pet a painless death. Don't leave your boxer alone at this moment. Pick up your pet and hold it tight; the dog will feel your touch and go peacefully to sleep.

Keep in Touch with Your Veterinarian

There are few diseases and illnesses to which your boxer is particularly prone. In these cases, only your veterinarian may help. Pay special attention to the following:
• **Pyloric stenosis** is a condition where the sphincter, a valve that controls the food flow from the stomach, is much too powerful and prevents any solid food from leaving the stomach. This condition is often seen in pups being weaned and presented with solids for the very first time. It can, however, also develop as a chronic problem in growing boxers.

Sign: Vomiting of solid food.

Treatment: Surgery.
• **Cushing's syndrome:** Due to an overactive adrenal gland, located near the kidneys, the boxer loses hair evenly on both sides of the body and legs and quickly gains a potbelly. This syndrome is often seen in boxers eight years or older. Boxers that are on long-term corticosteroid therapy can also develop this syndrome.

Sign: Excessive thirst; weakness of the abdominal muscles.

Treatment: Veterinary care is necessary.
• **Cryptorchidism:** Both testicles or testes should be present in the scrotum of a puppy by six to ten months of age.

If the play of its ribs is clearly visible, the boxer is not overweight.

Some breeds, among them the boxer, show an increased incidence of the condition known as cryptorchidism, when one or both testicles fail to descend to the scrotum. It is important that a male dog has two fully descended testes. If this is not the case, such a dog is called a "cryptorchid."

The testes inside an unborn puppy are attached to the scrotum by a ligament that contracts after the birth of the animal, causing the testicles to descend through the so-called inguinal canal into the scrotum. This process takes about two weeks, and after that time the testes can often be felt. However, as the puppy grows, fat in the scrotum often makes it difficult to feel the testes for a while, but this changes again after approximately four months.

Cryptorchids should obviously never be used for breeding, as cryptorchidism may be inherited by the offspring, although an implant of testosterone could help the male dog.

Treatment: The veterinarian will remove the retained testis surgically. Retained testicles are prone to cancer.

• **Proctosed globe** (eyeball bulges out of its socket) commonly occurs in all so-called brachycephalic dog breeds, like pugs and boxers. Immediate veterinary care is essential. If the eyeball remains exposed for a long period of time, the cornea will dry out and it may be impossible for the veterinarian to save the eye.

Treatment (first aid): Apply ophthalmic eyewash to keep the cornea moist at all times. Don't use tap water or anything that is not the right osmotic concentration. As soon as possible, get to the veterinarian, who will quickly replace the eyeball in the socket.

HOW-TO:
Health

If you suspect the presence of a disease, first check to see whether your boxer has fever or possibly a subnormal temperature. If your pet's temperature is below or above the normal range of 100.4 to 101.3° F (38–38.5° C), it is ill.

Taking the Dog's Temperature
Drawing 1

The generally accepted opinion that if a boxer's nose is hot it has fever is incorrect. The body temperature of a boxer can be reliably determined only by measuring it with a thermometer. It is a good idea to have someone help you perform the procedure. One person should hold the dog's head and speak to it soothingly while the other carefully inserts the thermometer into the rectum and holds it there until the reading is obtained. Lubricate the tip of the thermometer with some petroleum jelly beforehand.

Administering Medicine
Drawings 2 and 3

Tablets can be given to your boxer by concealing them in some liverwurst or ground beef. Some animals, however, then refuse to touch the food at all—even if the tablets are pulverized.

My tip: If that happens, open your boxer's mouth and push the tablet as far back into its throat as possible. Then hold its jaws shut until it has swallowed the medication.

Liquid medications are best given to your boxer with a disposable syringe, without the needle (see Drawing 2). Such syringes are available in pharmacies. Hold your boxer's head up, insert the syringe at one side of the dog's mouth, and slowly let the liquid trickle between its lip and teeth.

Powder: With the tip of your finger, place it on your pet's tongue or on the inside of its lip.

Suppositories have to be lubricated with some petroleum jelly before insertion. Push them as deeply as possible into the dog's rectum. You can wear a plastic glove for this procedure.

2) Let liquid medication trickle into the dog's mouth from one side.

Eye ointment and eyedrops should be placed inside the lower lid. To do so, pull the eyelid slightly downward (see Drawing 3).

Dressing Wounds
Drawing 4

Minor injuries: The dog will clean these itself by licking them, but you should keep an eye on these kinds of injuries as well, to ensure that no serious infection develops.

Profusely bleeding wounds have to be bandaged with a pressure dressing. First, using tweezers, try to remove all foreign bodies from the wound. Next, fold a piece of clean cloth to make a thick pad and press it against the bleeding wound. Then tie a scarf or a thin bandage around the affected part of the body.

Important: Heavily bleeding wounds on the legs require a second bandage, a tourniquet tied above the site of the injury. Loosen this bandage from time

1) Taking the dog's temperature is a job for two people: One person holds the boxer while the other inserts the thermometer.

to time, however, to allow blood to circulate in the leg. See the veterinarian immediately.

Wounds that are healing cause itching, and the boxer tries to deal with the problem by gnawing and biting at the spot. Ask your veterinarian how you can help your pet if that happens. The boxer also instinctively tries to remove bandages in order to lick its wounds. You need to prevent that by putting an Elizabethan collar on your pet (see Drawing 4).

Remedies for Insect Stings

The sting of a bee or a wasp, especially in the throat area, can place your boxer in mortal danger. Severe swellings in that area lead to difficulty in breathing and swallowing. Allergic reactions that cause circulatory disturbances are possible as well, however.

What to do: With every type of sting, the first step is to get your boxer calmed down. If it is a bee sting, remove the stinger if possible. Unusual reactions to a bee sting always require a trip to the veterinarian. Instant treatment by a veterinarian is absolutely imperative if a bee or a wasp has stung your boxer in the throat area. If it has been stung on the lip or some other body part or parts, you can give it a calcium ampoule and, in addition, cool down the affected area with cold compresses. You should always keep a supply of calcium ampoules on hand; they are available in pharmacies and pet supply stores.

Poisoning

The first symptoms of poisoning are severe vomiting, diarrhea, convulsions, circulatory collapse, labored breathing, severe irritation of the mucous membranes in the eye and throat areas, and possible blue coloration of the tongue.

What to do: Everything that is poisonous to your boxer should be kept out of its reach. If, despite all your precautions, your pet has ingested poisonous substances, take it to the veterinarian without delay.

Heatstroke

Boxers most commonly are affected by heatstroke, especially when they are old or fat, when left behind in a parked car in the broiling sun. Heatstroke also can occur in rooms without adequate ventilation or when the dog has physically overtaxed itself. These are the results:

• circulatory collapse
• weakness
• heavy panting accompanied by excessive drooling and a staring expression

3) Place eye ointment on the inside of the lower lid.

• fast-pounding pulse
• rise in body temperature (over 106° F [41° C])

What to do: If these symptoms appear, place damp cloths around your boxer's body; they are most effective in the head area. Carry the dog into the shade. Take its body temperature. The dog has to be examined by a veterinarian, even if its condition has improved.

Transportation to the Veterinarian

If you transport your boxer to the veterinarian's office in a car, you should have a dog carrier in the vehicle. In the absence of such a carrier, it is wise to have another person ride with you. During the trip, your companion can look after the dog in the back seat and keep it calm. If the boxer is seriously injured, contact the veterinarian before bringing in your pet. He or she will tell you the best way to transport the dog.

4) An Elizabethan collar will keep the boxer from removing bandages.

Breeding Boxers

Breeding boxers means steadily and continually improving the breed. If you decide to breed a female, or bitch, you have to be well acquainted with the breed characteristics and the breeding regulations (see The AKC Breed Standard, page 6). Moreover, you should belong to a breeders' club or association and adhere to their breeding regulations as well. An additional prerequisite for breeding is perfect health on the part of both breeding partners.

The right stud: In choosing the stud, not only its outward appearance—that is, its conformation—but also its temperament (see The AKC Breed Standard, page 6) is a factor.

Fitness for breeding is determined not only by physical characteristics, but also by the animal's temperament.

The Mating Act

Heat: The mating season begins with the estrual cycle of the bitch. A normally developed female first comes into season between her ninth and twelfth months of life. Every subsequent heat occurs at intervals of about seven months and lasts roughly 21 days. The minimum age at which a bitch may be bred is 18 months, according to the breeding regulations.

Readiness to mate: The heat begins with the swelling of the vagina and a bloody discharge. The bitch urinates more frequently and often does not squat so low during urination. It is important to make a note of the day when the bloody discharge first appears, because it is used to determine the period of time during which the bitch is willing to accept the attentions of a male. This phase begins on about the tenth day of the cycle and lasts six to seven days.

Mating act: Copulation usually is preceded by some preliminaries, typically including extensive sniffing of the sides of the neck and the ears. If that is followed by the actual mating act, both dogs remain "tied" together for some time. The tie may last 5 to 50 minutes.

Caution: During this phase, make no attempt to separate the animals, because wrenching them apart by force can result in serious injuries.

My tip: While in heat, a bitch absolutely has to be put on a leash when taken for a walk. The males follow the scent of a bitch in season and mate with her when they find her, if she happens to be at the right point of the estrual cycle. In addition, the bitch herself, in that stage of the cycle, will be on the lookout for a suitor, and she will not be exactly choosy about whom she selects.

Gestation

First and second weeks: The estrual bleeding continues even after mating has taken place. The bleeding may also cease or intensify, but that is no indication of whether conception has occurred. In the first two weeks after her season has ended, a bitch, even if pregnant, shows scarcely any external signs. Many bitches, however, exhibit an increased need for sleep at the beginning of the gestation period. Nonetheless, they should continue to get sufficient exercise at this time.

Third and fourth weeks: After approximately three weeks, a pregnant

Playing with other dogs is a way for puppies to become socialized.

bitch may possibly vomit gall (bile) or mucus in the morning. That is no cause for concern, but merely a sign that her metabolism is adjusting to the changed conditions. It is also possible that she will eat somewhat more poorly at this time, and sometimes she will even lose a little weight.

My tip: Don't make the mistake of overfeeding your pet now. A slight weight loss in this situation is not a problem; excessive weight gain, however, is. The widespread view that a pregnant bitch has to eat more than usual is erroneous. Rather, she needs food of greater nutritive value, with a high vitamin and mineral content in particular.

Fifth to ninth weeks: In the fifth week of pregnancy, the bitch's girth begins to expand. She continues to need exercise, but the increased burden on her circulation and lungs has to be taken into account.

End of the gestation period: The normal gestation period of a boxer bitch lasts between 61 and 63 days. Slightly longer or shorter gestations are completely within the realm of possibility, however. If a bitch carries longer than 65 days, the veterinarian should be consulted.

Size of the litter: The average size of a boxer's litter is about seven puppies per whelping.

The Whelping Box

The bitch needs a whelping box for the delivery. It should be made of wood and measure at least 33 x 45 inches (84 x 114 cm). In addition, it has to be about 10 inches (25 cm) high in front and roughly 20 to 24 inches (51–61 cm) high at the sides. To create the effect of a cave, cover the box with a blanket or a lid. The covering you use has to be removable, however, so that you can lift it off temporarily during the warm months.

Guard rail: The interior of the box has to be provided with a guard rail. This strip of wood, about 3 to 4 inches (8–10 cm) thick, should be attached around the circumference of the entire box, about 6 inches (15 cm) from the bottom. It will keep the puppies from getting trapped or even squashed between the mother dog and the walls of the whelping box.

Furnishings: Various materials can be used to make a bed for the puppies. They include needled felt and the so-called vet-drybed available commercially. For the whelping phase, you need to provide a moisture-proof pad, which you should cover well with absorbent paper.

The Whelping Process

The surest sign of impending labor is the dropping of the bitch's body temperature by 2.7 to 3.6°F. A boxer's normal temperature usually is around 100°F (38°C). When whelping is imminent, the bitch becomes restless, starts to pant, and wants to urinate with great frequency. Often she also refuses to eat 12 to 24 hours before giving birth.

The whelping process itself begins with the premonitory pains, followed by the start of the final stage of labor, when the puppies are expelled. Each puppy is born in an amniotic sac with a placenta. The fetal membranes are torn open by the mother dog as she frees her offspring from the sac. The still-wet newborn triggers in its mother an impulse to lick. That stimulates not only the puppy's circulation, but also the activity of its digestive organs. The bitch consumes the sac and the placenta as she licks the puppy clean.

The Puppies' Development and Nutrition

First to third weeks of life: Shortly after birth, the puppies are defenseless, at the mercy of a host of pathogens. For this reason, their mother's milk is of enormous importance for the newborns. Along with it, a puppy ingests vital antibodies. In addition, this so-called colostrum also has a mildly laxative effect. The puppy drinks and immediately thereafter empties its bowel. The mother helps this process along by licking the puppy. As she does so, she consumes the waste matter, just as she did after the puppy was born.

The puppy's eyes remain closed for about the first 10 days, and the ears, for the first 12 days.

Puppies' individual personality traits can be read from their behavior.

Fourth to seventh weeks: Roughly as the third week of life ends, the so-called imprinting phase begins (see Developmental Phases, page 27).

Important: At this time, it is essential to spend a lot of time playing with the puppies. It is through hand contact that they sense their special person and imprint on him or her.

Eighth week of life: The most opportune time for the puppies to go to new homes is two months after their birth, at the beginning of the socialization phase (see Developmental Phases, page 27).

Pointer: Before being handed over to their buyers, the puppies first have to be wormed and given their first series of vaccinations (see What the Buyer Needs to Know, page 14).

Weight check: The daily weighing of the puppies should be a matter of course for you. In this way you can immediately detect developmental disturbances in individual animals, because they can be read from insufficient weight gain. If the entire litter is not gaining weight normally, however, the fault lies with the mother dog. If she has no organic defects, you, as the breeder, have to give the puppies extra food in this case. Sometimes that may be necessary as early as the third week after birth.

My tip: During this time, provide the mother as well with supplementary doses of vitamins and calcium.

Showing Your Boxer

Dog shows are conformation shows that give an overview of the current state of breeding programs. They usually are held outdoors in an area designated as the "ring." The individual boxers, in various age groupings and in accordance with their level of specialized training, are judged separately, according to sex and color, by conformation judges (see The AKC Breed Standard, page 6). The best of their class are awarded prizes, and their owners receive a certificate attesting to that fact.

Prerequisite: Participation in national as well as international conformation shows is open only to registered boxers. "Registered" means that your boxer is listed in the records of the American Kennel Club and often of the appropriate boxer club, which contain the breed lines of its ancestors as well those of boxers, for many decades, back to the beginning of the boxer breed (see Useful Addresses and Literature, page 60). A certain level of discipline and good training on the part of your boxer are required for appropriate showmanship. For example, you have to be able to show the conformation judge your dog's teeth. Leash training and obedience are equally indispensable. Without them, even judging the dog's gait is impossible. Boxers that react aggressively to every other dog or possibly even to humans will never excel in the ring. Only a good-tempered, beautiful dog that stands out from its competitors by virtue of its impressive behavior can captivate the judges. With head proudly lifted, it will raise itself to its full height to make as imposing an appearance as possible. Incidentally, every naturally talented boxer will display such behavior in the show ring.

But regardless of how many points your boxer earns at the show, for you, your dog should always be the best and most beautiful.

Useful Addresses and Literature

International Kennel Clubs

American Kennel Club
   51 Madison Avenue
   New York, New York 10038

Fédération Cynologique
Internationale
   Rue Leopold II
   Thuin, Belgium

Australian Kennel Club
   Royal Show Ground
   Ascot Vale
   Victoria, Australia

Canadian Kennel Club
   2150 Bloor Street
   Toronto, Ontario M6540
   Canada

The Kennel Club
   1-4 Clargis Street, Picadilly
   London, W7Y 8AB
   England

New Zealand Kennel Club
   P.O. Box 523
   Wellington, 1
   New Zealand

American Boxer Club*
   6310 Edward Drive
   Clinton, Maryland 29735-
   4135

*These addresses may change as new officers are elected. The latest listing can always be obtained from the American Kennel Club.

Information and Printed Material

American Boarding Kennel
Association
   4575 Galley Road, Suite 400A
   Colorado Springs, Colorado
   80915
(Publishes lists of approved boarding kennels)

American Society for the
Prevention of Cruelty to Animals
(ASPCA)
   441 East 92nd Street
   New York, New York 10128

American Veterinary Medical
Association
   930 North Meacham Road
   Schaumberg, Illinois 60173

Gaines TWT
   P.O. Box 8172
   Kankakee, Illinois 60901
(Publishes *Touring with Towser*, a directory of hotels and motels that accommodate guests with dogs.)

Humane Society of the United
States (HSUS)
   2100 L Street NW
   Washington, DC 20037

Books

In addition to the most recent edition of the official publication of the American Kennel Club, *The Complete Dog Book*, published by Howell Book House, New York, other suggestions include:

Alderton, David. *The Dog Care Manual*. Hauppauge, New York: Barron's Educational Series, Inc., 1986.

Baer, Ted. *Communicating with Your Dog*. Hauppauge, New York: Barron's Educational Series, Inc., 1989.

——. *How To Teach Your Old Dog New Tricks*. Hauppauge, New York: Barron's Educational Series, Inc., 1991.

Gordon, John F. *All About the Boxer*. London: Pelham Books Ltd, 1978.

Klever, Ulrich. *The Complete Book of Dog Care*. Hauppauge, New York: Barron's Educational Series, Inc., 1989.

Pinney, Chris C. *Guide to Home Pet Grooming*. Hauppauge, New York: Barron's Educational Series, Inc., 1990.

Ullmann, Hans. *The New Dog Handbook*. Hauppauge, New York: Barron's Educational Series, Inc., 1984.

Wrede, Barbara. *Civilizing Your Puppy*. Hauppauge, New York: Barron's Educational Series, Inc., 1992.

Health Insurance for Dogs

Veterinary Pet Insurance
For details, call toll-free:
1-800-872-7387

Index

Because boxers occasionally appear to be somewhat dreamy and absentminded, they are also known as the philosophers of the canine world.

The Author

Johanna Thiel has been a boxer owner for more than two decades. Since 1980 she has bred boxers under the kennel name "vom Breuleck," and since 1989 she has been a breeding supervisor in the Frankfurt/Main Group of the Boxer Club. Together with her husband, who is a teacher-trainer in the same organization, she has had a long series of extraordinary successes in breeding boxers.

About the Photographer

Christine Steimer has worked as a freelance photographer since 1985. In 1989 she began to specialize in animal photography, and since that time she has been employed by the periodical *Das Tier* (*The Animal*). In addition, she is a photo-journalist of a general nature.

Important Notes

This pet owner's manual tells the reader how to buy and care for a boxer. The author and the publisher consider it important to point out that the advice given in this book is meant primarily for normally developed puppies from a good breeder—that is, dogs of excellent physical health and good character traits.

Anyone who adopts a fully grown dog should be aware that the animal has already formed its basic impressions of human beings. The new owner should observe the dog very carefully, including its behavior toward humans, and should meet the previous owner. If the dog comes from an animal shelter, it may be possible to get some information on the dog's background and characteristics.

Some dogs, as a result of bad experiences with humans, behave in an unnatural manner or may even bite. Such dogs should be taken in only by experienced dog owners. Even well-trained and closely supervised dogs sometimes damage someone else's property or, even worse, cause an accident. It is in the owner's interest to have adequate insurance protection, and we strongly urge all dog owners to purchase a liability insurance policy that covers their pet.

In addition, make sure your dog gets all the necessary immunizations and is wormed periodically (see page 48); otherwise, the health of humans and animals alike is placed at risk. If your dog shows signs of illness, it is essential to consult a veterinarian. If you have questions about your own health, see your physician and tell him or her that you keep a dog.

The Cover Photos

Front cover: Boxer with white blaze on forehead and chest

Back cover: Boxer puppy offering its paw as a sign of trust

© Copyright 1996 by Barron's Educational Series, Inc.
The title of the German book is *Boxer*.
Translated from the German by Kathleen Luft.
First English language edition published in 1996 by Barron's Educational Series, Inc.
English translation © Copyright 1996 by Barron's Educational Series, Inc.

All rights reserved.
No part of this book may be reproduced in any form, by photostat, microfilm, xerography, or any other means, or incorporated into any information retrieval system, electronic or mechanical, without the written permission of the copyright owners.

Address all inquiries to:
Barron's Educational Series, Inc.
250 Wireless Boulevard
Hauppauge, New York 11788

Library of Congress Catalog Card No. 95-45230

International Standard Book Number 0-8120-9590-1

Library of Congress Cataloging-in-Publication Data
Thiel, Johanna.
　[Boxer. English]
　Boxers : everything about purchase, care, nutrition, breeding, behavior, and training / Johanna Thiel ; translated by Kathleen Luft ; with color photos by Christine Steimer ; drawings by Renate Holzner.
　　p.　cm.—(A Complete pet owner's manual)
　　Includes bibliographical references (p.　) and index.
　　ISBN 0-8120-9590-1
　　1. Boxers (Dogs) I. Title. II. Series.
SF429.B75T4813　　1996
636.7′3—dc20　　　　　　　　　　　　95-45230
　　　　　　　　　　　　　　　　　　　　　CIP

PRINTED IN HONG KONG

6789　　9955　　987654321

The way the two brindle boxer puppies play with their mother makes it clear: The best thing for puppies is to grow up with their mother and along with their littermates. In the first weeks of life they need the daily contact with one another and the warmth of their "nest." When you acquire a boxer, it should have spent at least the first two months of its life with its canine family.